THE FLOWER APPRECIATION SOCIETY

An A to Z of All Things Floral

ANNA DAY AND ELLIE JAUNCEY
ILLUSTRATED BY ANNA DAY

sphere

For our wonderful families

CONTENTS

INTRODUCTION

When we met six years ago, pouring pints together in our local pub, we immediately bonded over a shared love of flowers – but we never dreamt that it would be the start of such an incredible adventure. Now we are lucky enough to work with flowers every day, thanks to The Flower Appreciation Society – the floristry business we started in the back room of that very same pub. (For more about the origins of The Flower Appreciation Society, read our story on page 168.)

Our backgrounds in illustration (Anna) and textiles (Ellie) gave us a strong visual identity right from the beginning. Creating all of our own branding as well as putting together beautiful floral arrangements have always made us 'not your average florists', and here we present to you 'not your average floristry book'.

Our book is an appreciation of *all* things floral – not just bouquets and buttonholes, but lots of flowery stories and making ideas. We want to share with you everything we've learnt since we started The Flower Appreciation Society. We want this book to encourage you to play with flowers, to show you just some of the wonderful things you can do with them and to give you useful tips we have picked up along the way. Whether you are a bride-to-be, a budding florist or just simply love flowers, we hope there is something here for everybody.

HOW TO USE THE BOOK

We've set the book out alphabetically and included a detailed index to help you find your way around. Although some letters were more challenging than others, the A–Z structure allowed us to explore some of the less obvious flowery ideas, like the way water travels around a plant . . . thankfully this solved the 'X' problem!

Throughout the book you will find illustrations of our favourite flowers, foliage and herbs, which we use in our arrangements time and time again. Under each flower you'll find its British season (the months it's available when grown in the UK) to encourage buying seasonally and locally wherever possible. There are also imported versions of all the flowers featured in the book – they often have longer seasons and are available for much of the year, and can be found at wholesale markets around the country. All this information can also be found in the Year of Flowers (page 254) which provides a useful reference to anyone wanting to know what is currently in season.

We also feature 'How-To' guides to some of The Flower Appreciation Society's favourite arrangements, including step-by-step instructions with flower and colour suggestions. We describe the market we use and tell tales from our beloved market traders. There is advice on taking care of your flowers, ideas for weddings, Valentines and Mother's day. Oh, and bees, handcream and how to choose the perfect jam jar are also included!

In making this book we became master jugglers. The Flower Appreciation Society kept going as usual but we stole every opportunity we could to work on our book – photographing the flowers during the days and spending the long summer nights writing and illustrating.

This was the busiest and most flowery year of our lives. It has changed the way we look at the world of flowers, and we hope this book will do the same for you.

How to Make a Flowery 'A'

Flowery letters are often associated with funerals, but we like using them for all sorts of other occasions (big flowery initials are wonderful at weddings and parties). Here's how to make a 'not your average' flowery letter . . .

Buy a floristry foam letter (see suppliers list on page 271) and soak it in water until it has absorbed plenty. Once the foam has changed from grass green to very dark green, it is ready to use. Choose a good selection of medium-sized, bold-shaped flowers (dahlias, zinnias and roses are all good for this).

Here we have chosen blooms which are as wide as the foam, so that we only have to use one on each row, but you can use smaller flowers if you prefer and add two or more per row.

Choose your first flower and cut the stem to about 5cm. Place it in the foam. We would recommend starting at the top and working down. Continue adding the flowers until the foam is completely covered.

Ammi

SEASON: MAY–AUGUST

These lacy white flowers resemble turned-out umbrellas, with hundreds of dainty flowers adorning each spoke. Ammi are also known as bullwort or common bishop's weed and are in the *Umbelliferae* family. We love using it for its delicacy and wild hedgerow feel. Ammi can grow to over two metres tall, which makes it perfect for large arrangements.

Aquilegia

SEASON: JUNE–JULY

Aquilegia comes from the Latin word *Aquila*, which means 'eagle', because the flower is thought to resemble an eagle's foot. We think they look more like frilly lampshades, bells or even tropical insects. Another common name for the flower is granny's bonnet and, like the anemone, they are from the buttercup (*Ranunculaceae*) family.

We're thrilled whenever we see these delightful flowers at the market as they have a very short season. Aquilegia come in all sorts of colours: some of our favourites are the pale lemon yellow, fuchsia pink, peach, amethyst and midnight blue. Look out for the extraordinary two-tone varieties which have very defined markings. Be careful though, these flowers are incredibly fragile so handle with care!

Anatomy of a Flower

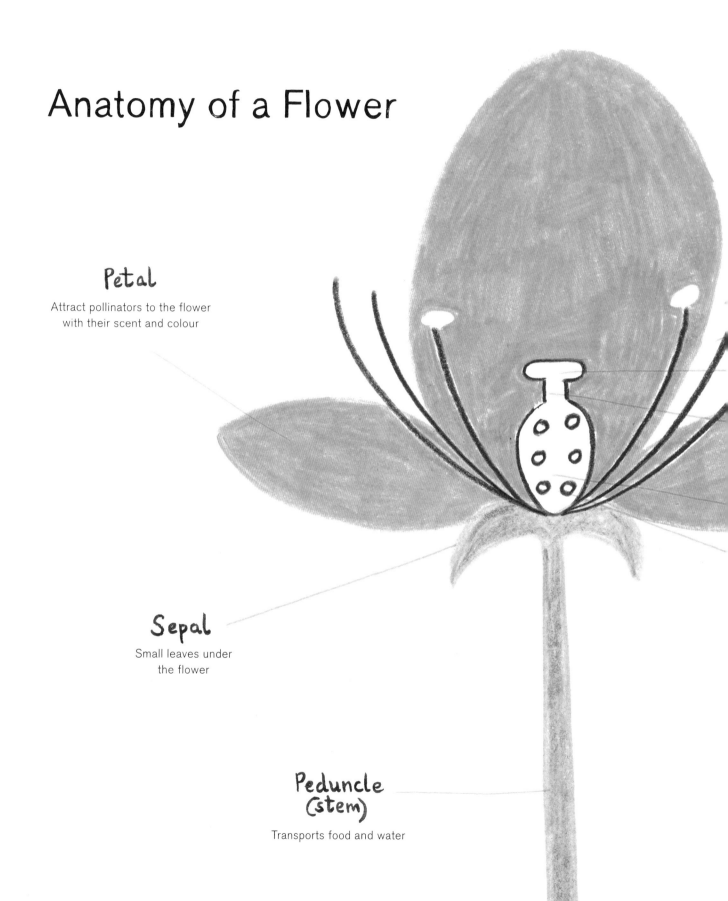

Petal
Attract pollinators to the flower with their scent and colour

Sepal
Small leaves under the flower

Peduncle (stem)
Transports food and water

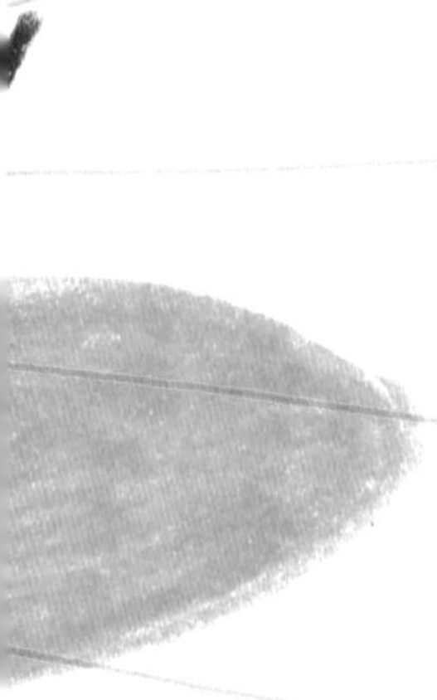

Anther

Female reproductive cells that will become the seed when fertilised by pollen

Filament

Holds and supports the anther

Stigma

Receives the pollen during fertilisation

Style

Tube on top of the ovary

Ovary

Female reproductive organ

Ovule

Female reproductive cells that will become the seed when fertilised by pollen

Stamen

Comprising the anther and the filament, this is the male organ of the flower

Pistil

The female organ of the flower, made up of the stigma, style and the ovary

20 · A

Astrantia

SEASON: MAY–OCTOBER

Ellie's granny used to call astrantia 'the melancholy gentleman'. The botanical name comes from *astron*, the Greek for 'star'. Bees and other pollinating insects love this beautiful stellar flower from the *Umbelliferae* family – even more than we do!

We always have astrantia on our shopping list – it works so well in arrangements we put it in almost everything. Its muted colours range from a silvery white or a very pale blush pink to a deep cerise. Watch out for its erratic wilting behaviour: sometimes astrantia is very strong and will be one of the last flowers in your vase still looking great, and other times it is weak and wilts very quickly. For this reason, when we use it in bridal bouquets we always trap it into the middle of the bunch so it is well supported.

A Trip to the Market

Florists work in all sorts of different ways: some buy directly from Holland (where many flowers are grown and the flower-distribution process begins); others, like us, go to the market, and those lucky florists who live in the countryside can buy straight from the grower. We buy the majority of our flowers from New Covent Garden Market in Vauxhall, London. We prefer the market, rather than buying directly from the Dutch sellers, because we like to handpick our flowers and see what we're getting. It gives us the opportunity to select the freshest, most beautiful blooms – and we love the buzz of the place.

For us, market days start at 5.30 a.m. Luckily we live just round the corner from each other, so picking the other up is not much of a detour for whoever's driving. Minutes are precious at that time of the day – especially in winter when it's still pitch black and feels like the middle of the night. We always bring a big coat and wear warm shoes, as even in the summer the market is kept cool for the flowers.

It takes us half an hour to drive through sleepy London – passing Smithfield's meat market en route, with bloody-aproned men carrying huge carcasses reminding us that we're not the only ones awake. Onwards we go, crossing the river just before the city's rush hour begins; it's one of Anna's most loved parts of the day. We get to the market for just after 6 a.m. The market actually opens around 4 a.m., so you can go earlier if you're feeling brave and have a lot to buy. The market begins to wind down at about 9 a.m. before closing its doors at ten o'clock, so if you're wanting to pick up a bargain bunch, or just want to browse, arriving later is fine. Anyone can go – it's free to get in, although there is a small parking charge.

There's a lot more to see at the market than just flowers and foliage: from mini pineapple plants to water features, to every kind of ribbon, wire, twine, floristry foam . . . every flower-related thing you could ever need. As for the flowers, make sure you have a good look around as a lot of the sellers have similar stock, and prices and quality may vary from stall to stall. You have to ask for prices and VAT is not included, so be conscious of this so you don't get a shock when paying! Bear in mind most flowers are sold in wraps of at least ten stems, so it's not the right place for buying in really small quantities.

We finish at around 9 a.m., our van filled with boxes and boxes of flowers. On our drive home we pass the army of city workers marching across London Bridge, starting their day. First things first when we get back to our studio: a strong cup of coffee before the unpacking begins.

Anemone

SEASON: MARCH–MAY

Anemones, one of the first spring flowers, come most often in gorgeous jewelly colours such as royal purple, ruby red, bright magenta and dark grape – it's always a joy to find some colour after a long winter. As well as these opulent colours, there are also subtler versions in snowy white and a lovely pale blush. Keep an eye out for the striking white anemone with a black centre – one of our favourites – and the beautiful cream-coloured ones, which have an amazing, almost painted, red stripe on them.

Anemones are also in the buttercup family, otherwise known as the buttercup family. There are over seventy varieties, but the one that is most commonly available at the market is the poppy anemone, or the *Anemone coronaria*. We like to remove the scruffy collar-like leaves which are about a quarter of the way down the stem before using them. Anemones continue to grow in the vase, so try cutting them a bit shorter than everything else in your bunch to allow for this. Or you might like to watch them grow!

Flowery Bonnet

A couple of years ago we were asked if we would like to go to Port Eliot festival in Cornwall to make real flower headdresses for the festival goers. We had no idea how popular this would be, and how wonderful they would look on everyone, young and old. The headdresses have now become one of our signature creations. Be it full flower bonnets, Frida Kahlo-esque front-facing head dresses, a little something on the side, or ethereal flowery circlets. Turn to page 102 for a step-by-step guide to making your own floral headdress.

29 · B

Bridal Bouquet

HOW TO MAKE A BRIDAL BOUQUET

The style of bridal bouquets has changed dramatically over the years, from simple posies to the tumbling waterfall bouquets favoured by brides in the eighties. (Princess Diana's extravagant bouquet is a perfect example of this.) Nowadays the brides we meet usually request a less structured wedding-day look, without too much cascading floral pomp.

The key to making a beautiful bridal bouquet (or bridesmaid bouquet) is in the flowers you choose. We make sure that we have an assortment of different sizes, shapes and textures before we begin. We like to use a mixture of flowers in our bouquets, but if you wanted to stick to one type (such as roses or peonies) the same rules apply.

Sometimes we make relaxed, wild bouquets and other times slightly neater versions.

You Will Need:

Floristry scissors, twine, ribbon and pins.

Flowers We Have Used:

Peonies, stocks, dahlias, hellebores, garden roses, astrantia, wild sweet peas and scabious.

step 1

Select a mixture of different-sized flowers. It's good to choose slim-stemmed flowers as these are easier to hold and to avoid very large blooms, such as hydrangeas, as these can be tricky to handle and will take up a lot of room in the bouquet.

Strip all the leaves on the stems and make sure you remove all thorns, as this is a hand-held bouquet! (See page 54 for tips on how to prepare your flowers for use.)

step 2

Neatly place all flowers in front of you; we like to separate the different blooms into groups so that it is easy to select them.

Pick a prominent flower (here we have used a peony) and place in your left hand (reverse if you are left-handed).

step 3

Now choose a different colour and shaped flower and place it on top of the first at a slight diagonal. As you start to add flowers the tendency is to clutch them tightly. Try to relax your hand, holding the flowers loosely. This will prevent them from bruising and will allow you to reposition the flowers, pulling them up higher or down lower if necessary.

step 4

Continue adding your flowers at a slight diagonal in the same direction, varying the flower choice and trying to avoid two of the same flowers sitting too close together. Every few stems turn the bouquet using your free hand so that you are conscious of what is happening at each angle. The stems will form a twist – the name for this is spiralling, and it helps to protect the stems from breaking. Trap any flowers that are prone to wilting (usually the softer-stemmed varieties like mint and astrantia) nearer the centre of the bunch so they are supported by hardier stems.

step 5

Stop when you are happy with the shape and size of your bouquet. A good way of checking this is to look in a mirror. If the bunch is looking slightly lopsided then add or take away flowers as you see fit. This is also a good time to loosen your grip on the bouquet, carefully pulling any blooms up which may have slipped down and are now hiding in the bunch.

step 6

Cut the stems so that the bouquet measures roughly 30cm in height (from top to bottom).

step 7

Twist a piece of twine (roughly 10cm) around the stems, where your hand has been holding the flowers, to secure the bunch.

step 8

Wrap a piece of ribbon (about 30cm in length) around the stems until 5cm remains.

step 9

Fold the end of the ribbon under itself to create a neat edge. To secure the ribbon, take three pins, pushing each one through the ribbon at a slight angle spread out equally along the ribbon's edge (making sure it doesn't pop out the other side, pricking you!). Alternatively you can cut a longer length of wide ribbon (roughly 150cm) and wrap it around the stems a few times. Tie in a big blousey bow and leave the ends hanging loosely.

step 10

To keep it fresh until you are ready to go, place the bouquet in a large jar filled with water, making sure the ribbon doesn't get wet.

The next page is a selection of our favourite bridal bouquets which we hope will inspire you to make your own.

We Appreciate These Boxes

Our flowers come in these rectangular boxes, expertly
packed at the market. They are re-used time and time again.
We love their nostalgic logos, many of which were designed
in the 1970s. Here are some of our favourites . . .

ENGLISH
FLOWERS

Bridesmaid Bouquets

COLOUR AND FLOWER INSPIRATION

Our bridesmaid posies tend to be mini versions of our bridal bouquets. Often we use slightly fewer colours and smaller flowers to distinguish the two, but the same techniques apply when making.

Have a look below for some bridesmaid bouquet inspiration . . .

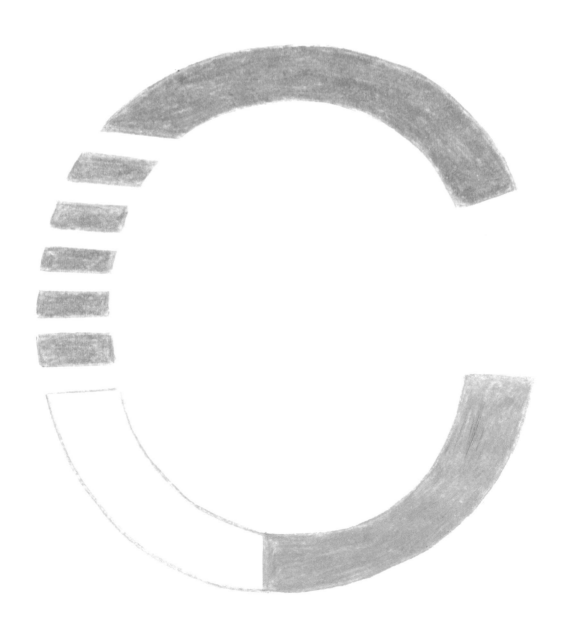

Clematis

The clematis we buy at the market is very different to the climber that you see scaling garden walls. It is cultivated so that it has long straight stems with a cluster of green leaves surrounding the bell-shaped blooms. Clematis is ideal for bouquets as not only do the flowers congregate at the top of the stem, but their leaves add a lovely touch of rich green to your flowery bunch. Clematis is in the buttercup family and the most common colour is a true purple, although sometimes you can get a lovely pale lilac or raspberry pink.

43 · C

Confetti

Fresh petal confetti is a fantastic alternative to the shop-bought, paper variety. It's equally effective with a mix of vibrant shades and shapes or with just one statement colour. Flowers which work particularly well are roses (both the single-headed variety as well as spray), individual delphinium heads and sweet peas. Fresh confetti is best prepared on the big day, but the petals will be fine if you prepare them the day before and store them in the fridge overnight. Making confetti is a lovely simple job for someone at a loose end on the wedding morning: pluck the petals from the flowers and place into a container/basket/paper cone – we use large pickle jars – the ones pictured hold roughly thirty handfuls of confetti.

A word of warning:

Some venues can be funny about confetti so it's good to check beforehand that it's okay to throw it. Dark petals can stain so you may want to stick to paler colours to avoid wedding-day disasters . . .

46 · C

Cornflower

SEASON: MAY–AUGUST

Cornflowers (*Centaurea cyanus*) are otherwise known as bluebottles or bachelor's buttons and are in the *Compositae* (daisy) family. They have fluffy petals and flimsy stems and are one of the few flowers at the market (as well as delphiniums and anemones) that come in a vibrant cobalt blue. They are also sometimes available in pink and a dark purple. Carefully remove their long, feathery leaves if they are looking tatty. Cornflowers are perfect for putting in jam jars and, as they can be edible*, for decorating cakes!

Make sure you buy them from an edible-flower supplier so you know they are safe to eat.

Cut-Glass Vases

COLOUR AND FLOWER INSPIRATION

Cosmos

SEASON: JUNE – SEPTEMBER

Here's another pretty flower from the daisy family. Available in candy colours with bright yellow centres, these grow tall and are multiple headed – great value for money. Simple in shape and design, they remind us of a child's drawing of a flower. Use them in all sizes of arrangements, adding them last because of their delicacy. Watch out for the petals, which are fragile and can bruise easily.

Cake Flowers

NOT YOUR AVERAGE CAKE STAND

While on the hunt for new ways to decorate cakes with flowers we came up with this simple idea…

Take two single-tiered cake stands and place one on top of the other. There will be a gap in between the two stands which you will eventually fill with flowers. Cut chunks of soaked floristry foam to fit the size of this gap and wedge them in. Stick a selection of marvellous blooms of all shapes and sizes into the foam, covering it completely in a floral blanket. Then simply place your cake on the top stand – not only will your flowers stay fresh all day but they also won't get in the way of cutting the cake!

A cake stand doesn't only have to be for cakes:

Try placing a colourful jelly, stack of profiteroles or a pineapple on top of the stand. If fake flowers are easier to get hold of, use them instead of real ones.

Conditioning

The first thing Anna learnt on her floristry course was the term 'conditioning' – nothing to do with washing your hair! Conditioning is the process of preparing your flowers for use and is the vital first step for any flower lover. It will help to make your flowers last, looking great for longer. See below for our top conditioning tips.

Always clean buckets and vases well using soapy water before use. For those pesky vases with narrow necks and hard-to-clean corners, a glug of thinned bleach from time to time works wonders.

In preparation for your flowers, fill your clean buckets up with cold water.

Take off all packaging that hold your flowers together, including twine and elastic bands. Often roses come with soft foam cases, protecting their heads, and hydrangea stems sit in little plastic water bubbles, or their own mini test tubes for a drink in transit. Make sure you carefully remove all of the above.

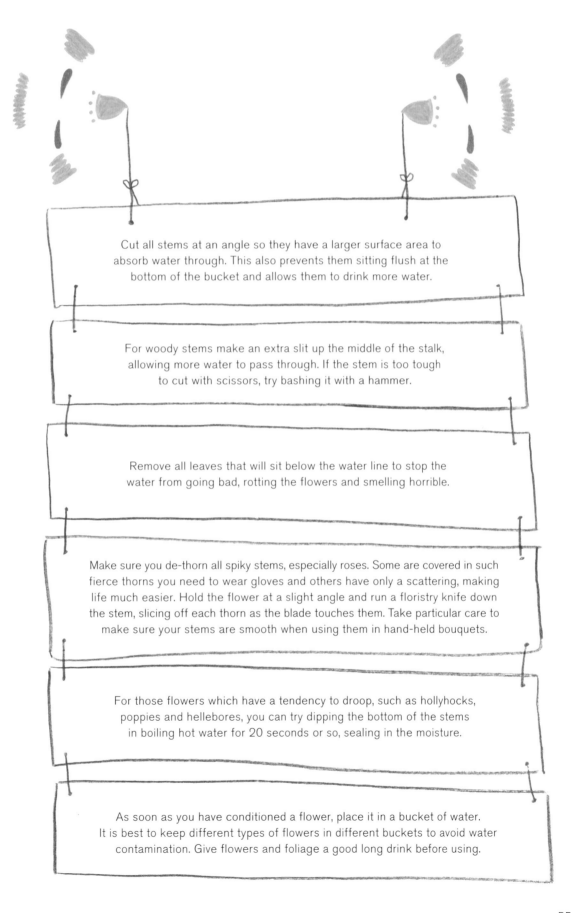

Cut all stems at an angle so they have a larger surface area to absorb water through. This also prevents them sitting flush at the bottom of the bucket and allows them to drink more water.

For woody stems make an extra slit up the middle of the stalk, allowing more water to pass through. If the stem is too tough to cut with scissors, try bashing it with a hammer.

Remove all leaves that will sit below the water line to stop the water from going bad, rotting the flowers and smelling horrible.

Make sure you de-thorn all spiky stems, especially roses. Some are covered in such fierce thorns you need to wear gloves and others have only a scattering, making life much easier. Hold the flower at a slight angle and run a floristry knife down the stem, slicing off each thorn as the blade touches them. Take particular care to make sure your stems are smooth when using them in hand-held bouquets.

For those flowers which have a tendency to droop, such as hollyhocks, poppies and hellebores, you can try dipping the bottom of the stems in boiling hot water for 20 seconds or so, sealing in the moisture.

As soon as you have conditioned a flower, place it in a bucket of water. It is best to keep different types of flowers in different buckets to avoid water contamination. Give flowers and foliage a good long drink before using.

Delphiniums

SEASON: MAY–AUGUST

The word delphinium comes from the Greek *delphis*, which means dolphin, because the flower spur is said to resemble a dolphin's head. These pointed, long-stemmed beauties from the buttercup family are lifesavers in large arrangements – a bunch of delphiniums can go a very long way.

Delphiniums come in a variety of cool colours: brilliant white, the palest of lilacs, sky blue, royal blue and an iridescent purple. A single stem will sit proudly in a glass bottle, which looks fantastic repeated along a windowsill. The individual flower heads are also perfect for confetti (see page 44–5). However, they are not so great in hand-tied bouquets or low arrangements as you would need to remove the bottom half of the flowers covering the stem, which is a real shame.

Cornflower

Nasturtium

Chive flower

Viola

Borage

Dianthus

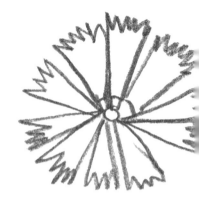

Delicious Flowers

Here are our favourite edible flowers,
try using them in the following ways . . .

Scatter a punnet of colourful, mixed edible flowers on
top of a cake, instantly transforming a boring sponge into
a feast for the eyes.

Stick them in jelly – why not try raspberry, gin and violet,
or elderflower and geranium jelly?

Freeze borage flowers in your ice tray with water for a
glorious surprise at the bottom of your glass.

Add nasturtiums and cornflowers to brighten up any salad.

Mix chive flowers into your mayonnaise and serve with
potatoes and a lovely piece of grilled fish.

Derek's Edible Flower Punnets

Make sure you buy from a reputable edible flower source so that they are grown especially for your consumption!

We order ours online from our specialist edible flower grower, Derek (see suppliers list, page 271). We explain to him the colour palette and our taste requirements and in the next post we receive our delicious floral package. Oh, what a lovely transaction!

Dahlias

SEASON: JULY– OCTOBER

Dahlias are full of character, from spiky prongs, to tightly packed pompoms, to perfect water lily shapes. We buy these show-stopping blooms by the bucket. Within each bucket there is a firework display of colour: neon yellow, acid orange, perfect peach, blood red, bubblegum pink, dark aubergine, nearly black. The only colour left out seems to be blue.

Originally wild flowers from Mexico, dahlias also belong to the daisy family. These late-summer blooms are wonderful in all sizes of arrangement but beware, their lifespan is short, perhaps because of their splendour. Look out for the giant dahlias which measure an unbelievable 25cm wide, straight from an old Dutch painting.

The way we buy flowers in the UK has changed significantly in recent years. In the 1970s we grew over 50% of our own flowers in Britain. Today we produce around 10% – mostly daffodils. This dramatic shift is because we now import cut flowers from all over the world. New varieties and choices are available all year round, which make buying flowers more exciting for everyone, but which comes with a significant environmental cost – farming, air miles and distribution, to mention the most obvious.

In 2013 we imported £660 million of cut flowers and exported a mere £26 million. People who buy cut flowers are becoming more conscious of the impact of importing flowers from far-off climes and are now starting to look more for locally grown produce, albeit on a smaller scale. There are networks such as Flowers from the Farm and The British Flower Collective who champion British cut flowers and help people connect with their local flower growers and florists around the country. We think this is a brilliant idea because it not only encourages people to buy fresh, seasonal flowers, but also locally grown ones. (See supplier list, page 271 for details).

We use British flowers and foliage as much as possible. There are a few sellers who specialise in locally grown flowers at the market. For foliage we use GB Foliage, who have a wide selection of greenery all year round, much of it sourced locally. Between May and October

we buy most of our English flowers from either Pratley or Zest. At Pratleys, boxes are stacked high, filled with scabious, delphiniums, dahlias, peonies, sweet peas and Solomon's seal. Twice a week Zest gets a delivery of beautiful English roses and a wide selection of wild meadowy flowers and herbs. These sit enticingly at the front of the stall in low buckets. Get to the market early if you want to buy English flowers as they get snapped up quickly! (See pages 254–63 for British flower seasons.)

We are also lucky enough to have found Bridget who has a wonderful garden in Oxfordshire. A few years ago she approached us with the exciting offer of supplying and delivering her flowers – a dream come true. Having chatted to her about the types of flowers we like to use, and listening to her recommendations, all we have to do now is to suggest colours and she will deliver an incredible selection of cut flowers to our studio – things we never see at the market. Last year our favourite new additions were didiscus and Japanese anemones.

Whether they have been picked from a garden or grown commercially, British blooms have an entirely different quality to those that have been especially cultivated in far-flung countries and made to endure long flights and cold fridges. We want to support British growers and prefer to use these delicate, sweet-scented, locally grown flowers whenever possible.

Which One Is Which?

We wanted to show you the difference between an arrangement made entirely from imported flowers and one that includes the same imported flowers with English garden flowers added. The urn on the left has stocks, sweetpeas, roses, scabious, dahlias, astrantia and peonies, all bought at the market. We use the very same flowers for the urn on the right but have added English aquilegia, philadelphus, honeysuckle, *Orlaya grandiflora*, pink geranium, sweet rocket and cat mint (all from Bridget's garden).

We love to include wild or garden flowers in any arrangement because of the delicacy and interest that they add (as well as a glorious scent). If you have access to a garden, hedgerow, or even a window box, add a few flowers, sprigs of greenery, or herbs to give your arrangement a completely different feel.

Earrings

HOW TO MAKE A FLOWERY EARRING

If headdresses are not really your thing but you still want to add a flowery touch to your outfit, why not try making real flower earrings? Carnations, spray roses, a section of a hydrangea's head and scabious are all good, hardy-stemmed flowers to use.

Flowery earrings look great with more than one bloom, so play around with stacking a few on top of each other and changing the directions that the flower heads face.

You Will Need:

Scissors, wire, earring hooks (easy and cheap to buy online).

Flowers We Have Used:

Two carnations.

step 1

Cut the stem, about half an inch away from the head of the flower.

step 2

Thread half of the wire through the stem, underneath the flower head.

step 3

Twist the two halves of wire together to create one wire stem.

step 4

Thread the earring hook through the wire stem so that it sits underneath the flower head.

step 5

Twist the remaining wire around the stem and cut.

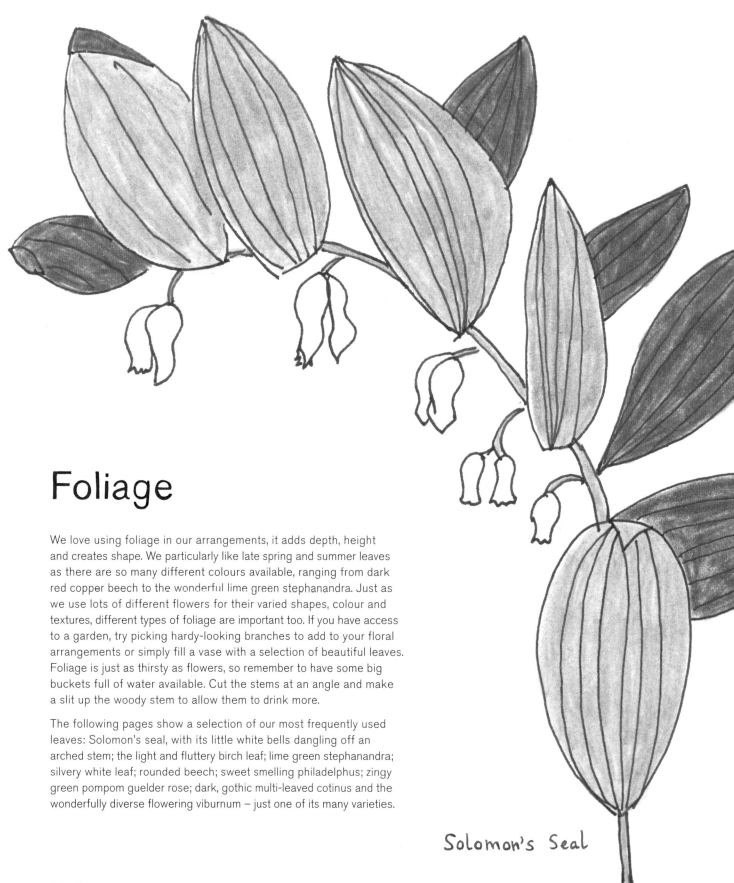

Foliage

We love using foliage in our arrangements, it adds depth, height and creates shape. We particularly like late spring and summer leaves as there are so many different colours available, ranging from dark red copper beech to the wonderful lime green stephanandra. Just as we use lots of different flowers for their varied shapes, colour and textures, different types of foliage are important too. If you have access to a garden, try picking hardy-looking branches to add to your floral arrangements or simply fill a vase with a selection of beautiful leaves. Foliage is just as thirsty as flowers, so remember to have some big buckets full of water available. Cut the stems at an angle and make a slit up the woody stem to allow them to drink more.

The following pages show a selection of our most frequently used leaves: Solomon's seal, with its little white bells dangling off an arched stem; the light and fluttery birch leaf; lime green stephanandra; silvery white leaf; rounded beech; sweet smelling philadelphus; zingy green pompom guelder rose; dark, gothic multi-leaved cotinus and the wonderfully diverse flowering viburnum – just one of its many varieties.

Solomon's Seal

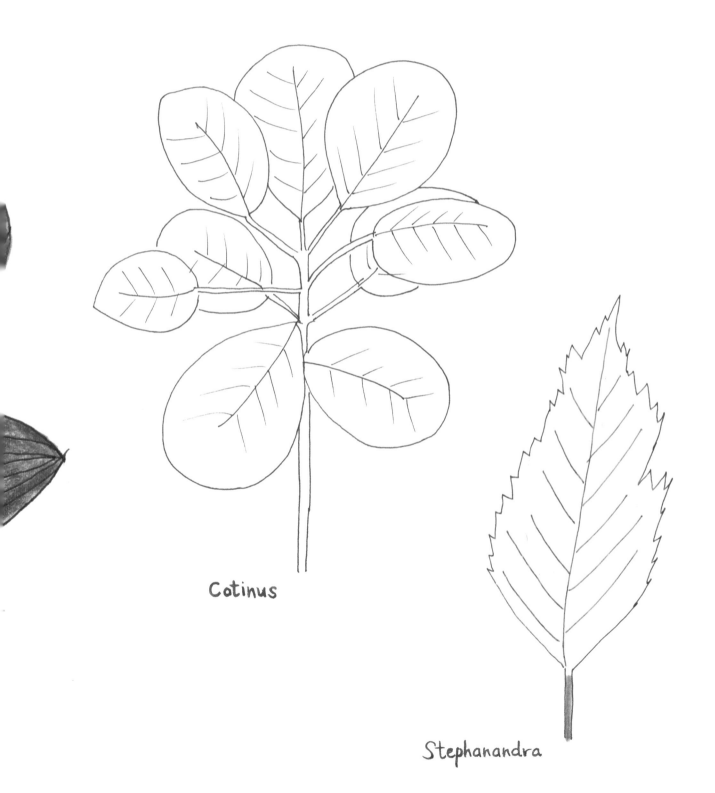

Cotinus

Stephanandra

Philadelphus

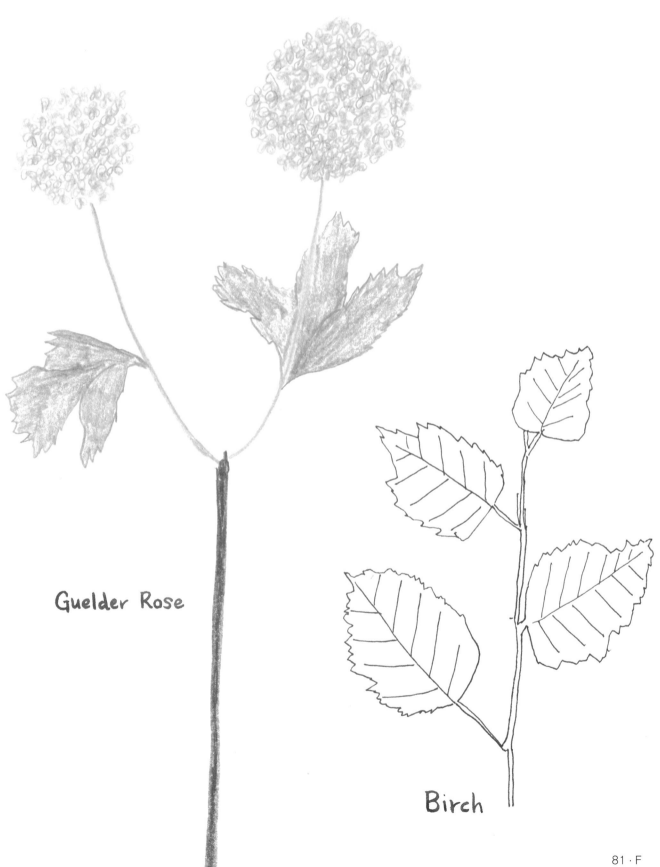

Guelder Rose

Birch

81 · F

White leaf

Beech

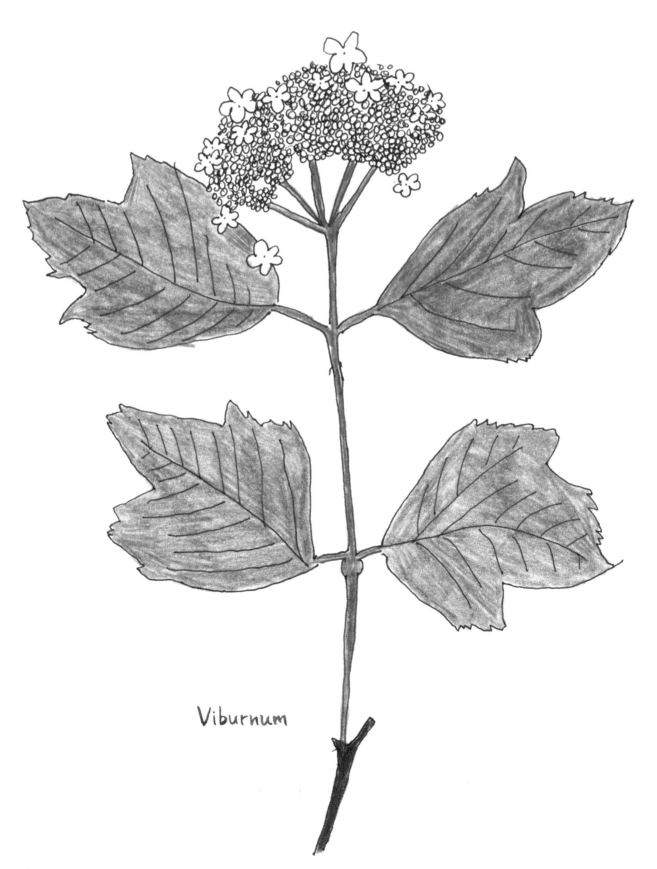

Viburnum

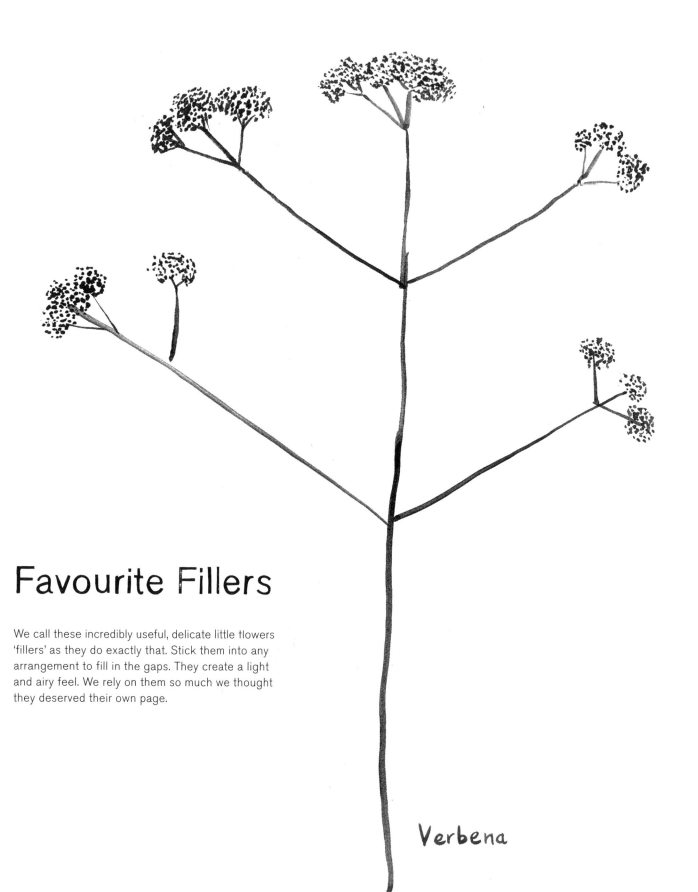

Favourite Fillers

We call these incredibly useful, delicate little flowers 'fillers' as they do exactly that. Stick them into any arrangement to fill in the gaps. They create a light and airy feel. We rely on them so much we thought they deserved their own page.

Verbena

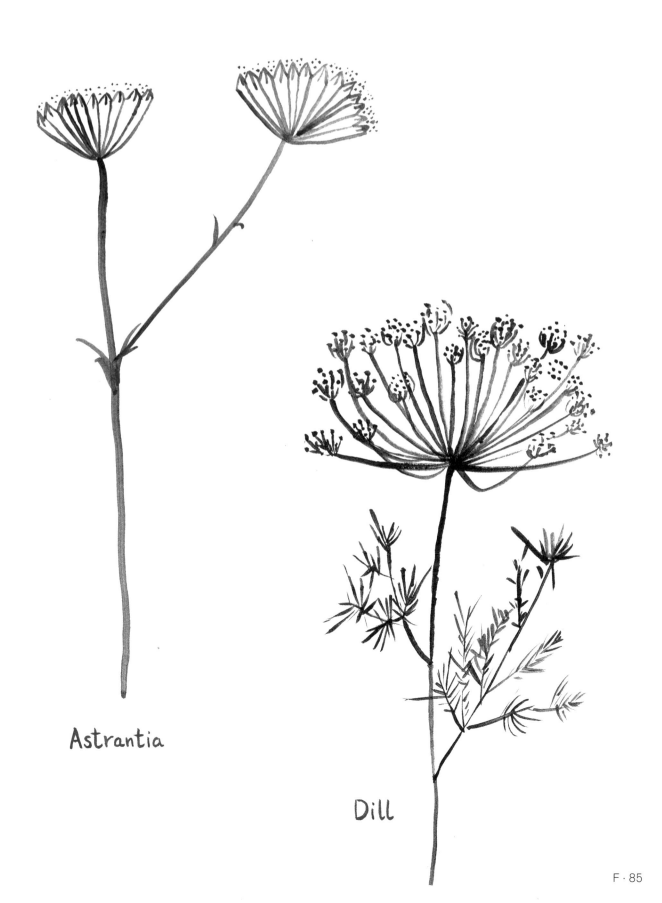

Astrantia

Dill

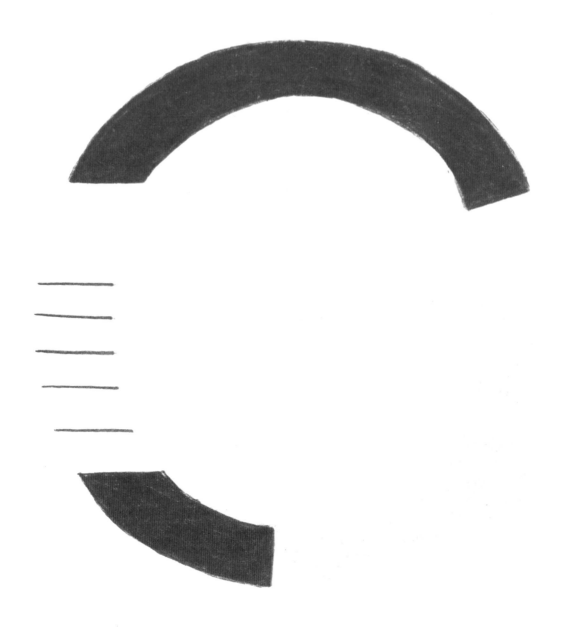

G · 87

GAS

Garage Flowers

Our inspiration has always been flowers that you might find in beautiful gardens or wild meadows. So we never dreamed we would find a use for your typical 'garage' flower until we discovered that they are absolutely perfect for our headdresses. There's no need to make a special and potentially expensive trip to the flower market or a florist. You can go to your local garage (or supermarket) and buy a selection of carnations, spray roses, freesias or chrysanthemums (all of which survive well out of water) and create a wonderful headdress. (See pages 102–3.)

Gold

Not Your Average Christmas Decoration

For florists, the Christmas season tends to involve a lot of rather traditional festive decorating, from pine cones to wreaths to cinnamon sticks and red ribbon. Last November Anna's sister got married and we were set the challenge of decorating the tables with a nod to the festive season, but avoiding reds and greens at all costs. We came up with this gold theme which worked really well.

Pineapple

Choose a pineapply-looking pineapple and cut a couple of centimetres off the base so that it sits flat and does not wobble. Spray gold (or another colour if you prefer) with a quality spray paint – do it outside and wear a mask. They look great on their own, or in a line running down the middle of a table, and will last a couple of days.

Palm

Choose a selection of palm leaves – we find the spindly kentia palms work best. Spray both sides of the leaf to give an even layer of colour, taking the same precautions as with the pineapple. For a winter wedding, tie a couple together and attach them to a pew end – fronds facing up. Or place three or four in a vase, fanned out. (Use floristry foam for stability if necessary.) These can also be turned into bunting: use a needle to run a thread through the stems of the palm leaves, so the fronds hang down. Repeat, creating a long line of golden waves.

Other things that look great sprayed gold or silver (or why not try some pastel shades?) are artichokes, poppy seed heads, dried hydrangeas and pine cones.

Appreciate a Groom

HOW TO MAKE A BUTTONHOLE

We make each of our buttonholes look a little different.

Flower selection is of the utmost importance as they have to endure a whole day of thirst and hearty hugs.

We recommend using hardy stems. Spray roses are perfect for this: small-headed, long-lasting and great value for money. Mix them with interesting herbs and foliage such as fresh or dried lavender, heather, rosemary, pittosporum, wax flowers, olive leaves and senecio. This will give a lovely fragrance and wild feel. We also like to add slightly more fragile flowers like astrantia, clematis, scabious, dill and the tips of delphiniums. Make sure you place these behind the sturdier flowers, trapping them in and preventing them from wilting.

If you can't get to a market or florist go to your local supermarket and buy a bunch of roses and a packet of rosemary. Add any sprigs of green you can find in the garden and follow the steps on this page.

Be sure to make your buttonholes on the morning of the wedding and keep them in water until you are ready to wear them. Just before you attach them, dry the ends with a towel. It's a lovely simple job for anyone in the wedding party who likes playing around with flowers.

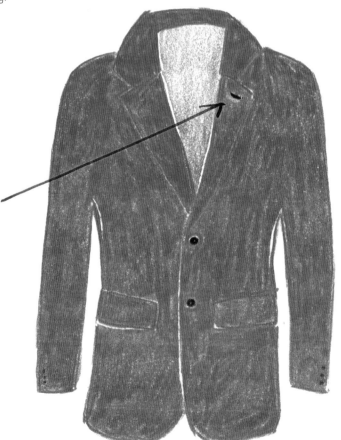

buttonhole goes here

You Will Need:
Gardening string, scissors, a pin.

Flowers We Have Used:
Spray roses, clematis, delphiniums, dried lavender, astrantia, pittosporum and senecio.

step 1

Choose a selection of hardy-stemmed flowers, herbs and foliage. Group these together in a balanced shape making sure that the foliage and herbs sit behind the flowers.

step 2

Cut the stems to about 8cm long.

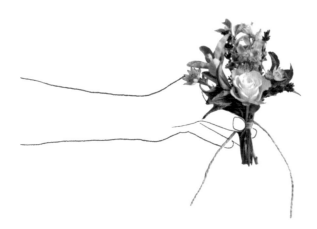

step 3

Cut a piece of string about 20cm long and wrap tightly around the stems of the flowers. Fasten with a knot and trim.

step 4

Finish by poking a pin through the tied string, ready to stick to the jacket.

Hellebores

SEASON: NOVEMBER–APRIL

Also known as the Christmas rose, hellebores (*helleborus*)
come in a variety of lovely muted tones, from very pale blush pink,
to gold to dark dusty burgundy and belong to the buttercup family.
Hellebores pop up in the depths of winter, adding a delightful
garden feel to any arrangement. They can however be rather hit
and miss: the perkiest-looking head can wilt very quickly, and
there doesn't seem to be any way of knowing which ones will
behave this way. Our wonderful market trader Sonny gave us this
tip: wrap a bunch of hellebores tightly in a piece of newspaper
and cut the stems at an angle. Place the bunch in a tall vase with
about 20cm of cold water in it. Leave them to sit for a few hours
before you use them. We find this works brilliantly, give it a go!

Hollyhocks

SEASON: JULY–AUGUST

These towering summer flowers, with the botanical name *Alcea rosea*, stand proudly in many gardens, sometimes reaching over three metres tall. The apricot colour is our favourite, but they also come in an array of other sunset shades. They are part of the *Malvaceae*, or mallow, family and look wonderful in large tall arrangements.

HEADDRESS

Headdress

How to Make a Flowery Headdress

We used to wire every individual stem onto the base of our headdresses, which made them heavy, scratchy and very time consuming. Three years later we had a eureka moment. We realised that we could replace the wire with floristry tape, which changed everything . . .

You Will Need:

Scissors, floristry tape, lightweight malleable wire (we use aluminium) and a selection of flowers (the hardier the stems, the longer they'll last).

Flowers We Have Used:

Hydrangeas, piaget roses, scabious and dahlias.

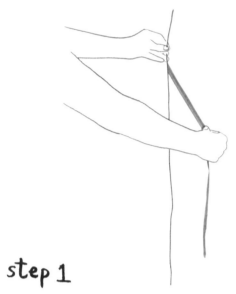

step 1

Cut the aluminium wire to a length that is slightly longer than your head's diameter. Cover the whole wire in floristry tape to give a neater finish. The trick is to stretch the tape diagonally and wrap it around the wire, squeezing as you go so that the tape sticks to itself. At this point, keep the wire straight.

step 2

Now take your first flower and cut the stem so that there is about 5cm left below the flower head. Using the floristry tape, bind the stem of the flower onto the wire.

step 3

Keep adding flowers in the same direction so that all the stems face the same way, and the next flower sits neatly on its predecessor's stem. Tightly packing the flowers helps to prevent them from wilting. When you are happy with your headdress, wrap it around your head making a circlet and twist the ends together securely.

Extra tips...

Make your headdress as close to the occasion as possible. These are wonderful but short-lived, one-night-only creations! For something longer lasting, try making your headdress with fake flowers.

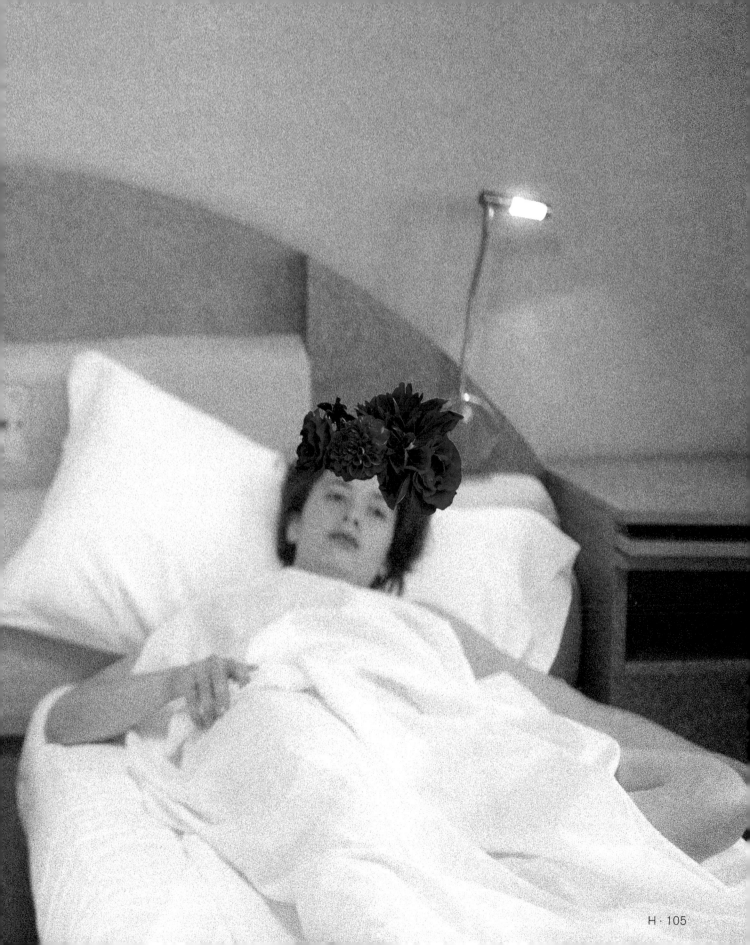

Herbs

For centuries people have used these aromatic, utilitarian plants. We have cooked, cleaned, anointed, perfumed and nursed with them. Today herbs are still widely used: rosemary with lamb, sage in stuffing, lavender in soap, mint in toothpaste . . . but don't forget that they look and smell wonderful in flower arrangements too.

Herbs are abundant in the summer months. We buy them from the market but you can also grow and pick them from your garden or window box.

Mint

Lavender

Rosemary

Oregano

Mint (*Mentha*) is our all-time favourite and adds a freshness in colour and scent to any arrangement. A selection of different varieties are available including Moroccan and Spearmint. It is susceptible to wilting so give it a good drink.

Rosemary (*Rosmarinus*) is our trusted buttonhole friend and has a much longer season than other herbs that we use. It is hardy and smells great, especially when crushed in a wedding-day hug!

Lavender (*Lavandula*) can be bought fresh or dried all year round. We use it a lot in the winter (dried), when fragrant herbs are scarce, and fresh in the summer when there is plenty available. This versatile herb is perfect for buttonholes, headdresses or just bunched together and placed in a bottle. (Keep an eye on the water as it has a tendency to turn yellow very quickly.)

Oregano (*Origanum*) comes in a variety of colours – white, lilac, dark purple and dark red. We love to use these fluffy flowerheads in bouquets.

These are only a few of the herbs that can be used in flower arranging. Try bay leaves, painted sage, flowering chives, flowering basil and salvia.

Appreciate Your Hands

Working with flowers takes its toll on your hands as they are exposed to the cold, and are often wet. You must look after these precious tools of the trade. We always have a tube of our favourite nourishing salve to hand. Ellie especially likes Kiehl's Ultimate Strength Handsalve. Anna's favourite is L'Occitane Shea Butter Hand Cream.

Some flowers and foliage have a tendency to irritate the skin. Watch out for the following: hellebores, hyacinths, daffodils, bluebells, narcissi, tulips, irises, euphorbia and ivy. Often these flowers contain white, watery sap in their stems so make sure you handle with care and wash your hands frequently. We would recommend wearing gloves if you have extra-sensitive skin.

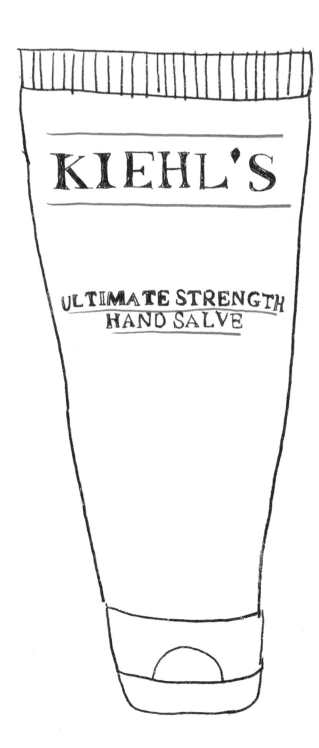

KIEHL'S

ULTIMATE STRENGTH
HAND SALVE

L'OCCITANE

CREME MAINS
20%
DRY SKIN
HAND CREAM

Ellie's favourite handcream

Anna's favourite handcream

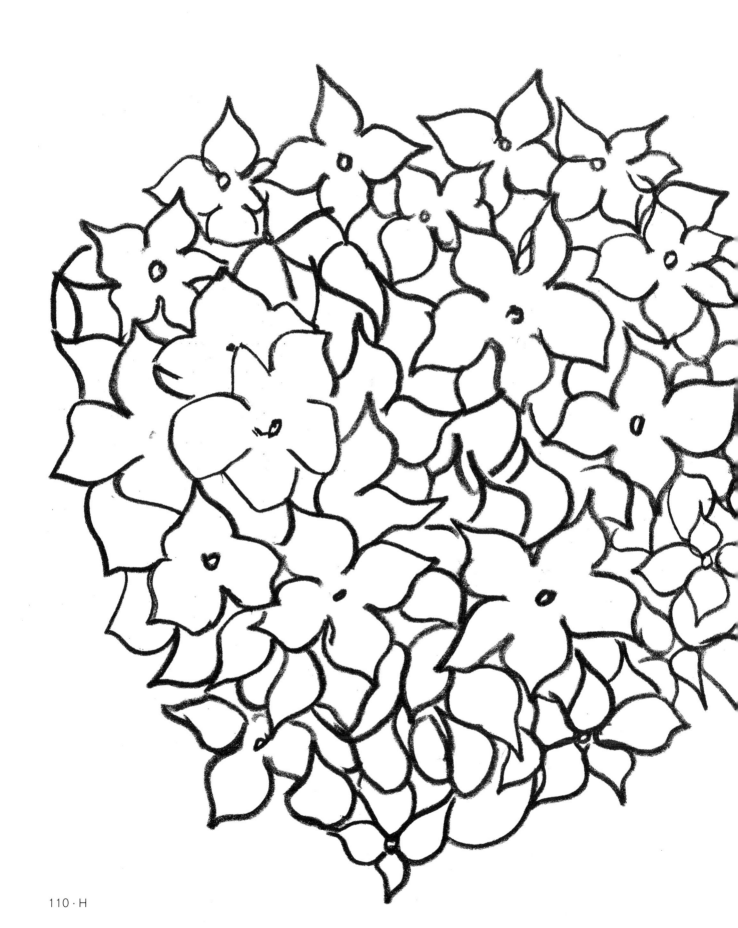

Hydrangeas

SEASON: JUNE–SEPTEMBER

Available from mid-summer to late autumn, they are in the *Hydrangeaceae* family. Throughout their season, the distinctive heads change colour on the bush. Beginning with lipstick pinks and baby blues, changing to subtle lilacs, sage greens and pearly pinks in late summer and finally developing into burnt reds and dark greens in the autumn.

The most common hydrangea that we see at the market is the aptly named mop-head variety. These rounded, voluptuous blooms perch on long straight stems, sitting like upside-down mops in their buckets. There are other types of hydrangeas that we like to use and buy whenever we see them. These include the various lacecap varieties, as well as Annabelle (*Hydrangea arborescens*) and Pink Diamond (*Hydrangea paniculata*). Hydrangeas can be temperamental – sometimes we find they keep their shape even when they have dried (great sprayed gold for Christmas decorations) – other times they wilt almost as soon as they come out of their packaging. We suggest putting them in a bucket of cold water immediately, giving them a good spray (again using cold water) and searing the ends. To sear the end you can either dip it in boiling water or hold it over a flame for a few seconds.

I LOVE YOU

'Roses are red . . .' but they also come in every shade of pink, lilac, yellow, white and cream. On Valentine's Day we encourage our customers to say 'I love you' a little differently. Here are some ideas for all of you out there who are also a little tired of the traditional red rose.

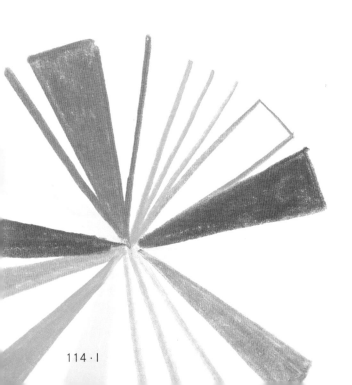

Appreciate Your Lover With...

A big bunch of red tulips – wrap in paper and tie with a silk bow.

Save an empty wine bottle from a special night you've spent together and put in it a beautiful single stem, like a shocking pink rose.

Make or buy a heart-shaped cake and sprinkle with rose petals.

If you can't get to a florist, buy a bunch of supermarket flowers and spruce them up: take off all their packaging and rewrap with some nice wrapping paper (or tissue paper, brown parcel paper or even newspaper). Tie with ribbon or a brightly coloured bit of string and make a lovely card to go with them.

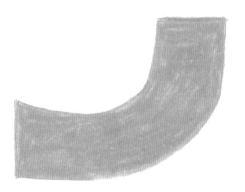

Jug

HOW TO FILL A JUG

We often use large jugs (roughly 30cm tall) for lovely informal arrangements. However the steps below can be applied to any size jug.

This jug is front facing, but you can make your jug arrangement equally beautiful on all sides by following these same steps but make sure you keep turning the jug so that you are building up your arrangement from all sides. It works well having the tallest stems in the middle.

You Will Need:

Scissors and a jug.

Flowers We Have Used:

Delphiniums, scabious, *Hydrangea paniculata*, lysimachia, hellebores, dill, lupins and roses.

step 1

Choose a jug and a selection of flowers and fillers. It's a good idea to choose big and small blooms, making sure there is a variety of shapes and textures. Include tall stems and avoid using anything which might be too short for your jug. We like to add some shades of green, whether that's foliage or fillers. Now condition your flowers and foliage (see pages 54–5). Lay your flowers, fillers and foliage out in front of you in neat piles.

step 2

Make sure your jug is clean and filled with cold water. Think about how tall you would like your arrangement to be. Measure your first tall-stemmed flower (we've used a delphinium) by holding it in front of the jug to see how much needs to be cut off. Repeat this method for every flower you are using, making sure you vary the heights.

step 3

Continue adding similar height flowers. We recommend using an odd number of each stem, especially with the prominent blooms – this tends to work better aesthetically.

step 4

Next add some big, some medium and some pointy flowers. (Here we have lysimachia, *Hydrangea paniculata*, lupins and roses.) The placement should be slightly random and not evenly spaced. Don't worry about gaps – you will fill these in later on.

step 5

Now place the smaller sized blooms in the jug (we've used scabious and hellebores) at varying heights.

step 6

Finally add your fillers (we've used dill) where needed. Turn over to see examples of our flowery filled jugs.

Jars

HOW TO CHOOSE THE PERFECT JAR

Jars and bottles make lovely vases and it is so satisfying to find another use for them long after the jam is finished and the wine has been drunk. We are constantly on the hunt for jars and forever grateful to our wonderful neighbour, Judith. Every week she delivers a bag of old jars (and usually a piece of cake) to our studio in return for our leftover flowers for her community café down the road.

Our search for the perfect jar means that our shopping trolley is often filled with a strange assortment of pickles, olives and rhubarb compote!

However, it's best to avoid short, squat jars as they take a lot of flowers to fill and it seems a shame to cut them down so low. Using bottles and narrow-necked jars is a great way to make flowers go further as you only need a few stems in each. Look out for lovely details: lines, squares, diamonds and other patterns etched into the glass. Bonne Maman jars are our favourite.

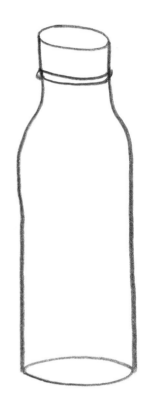

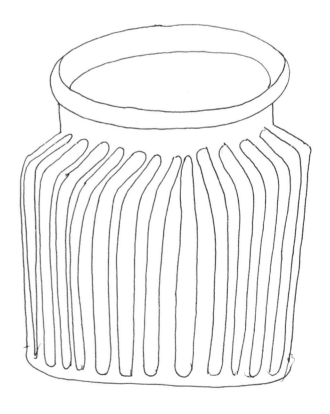

Jar

HOW TO FILL A JAR

Jars are a great vessel to fill with flowers as you often have them lying around the house and it's a nice way to recycle them. Follow our seven quick steps below and fill a jar with lovely flowers . . .

You Will Need:

Scissors and a jar.

Flowers We Have Used:

Peonies, astrantia, dahlias, stocks, wild sweet peas, hellebores, mint and scabious.

step 1

Choose a selection of flowers in all different shapes and sizes. Strip all leaves and thorns that might sit below the water level (see page 55).

Find a nice shaped jar (see pages 124–5) and fill almost to the brim with cold water.

step 2

Lay your flowers out in neat groups so you can see what you have got to work with. Select a medium-sized bloom to start with and place in your left hand (the reverse if you are left-handed).

step 3

Now choose a different colour and shape flower and place on top of the first at a slight diagonal. Keep your hand relaxed as you gather the flowers, holding them gently – this will prevent them from squashing and will allow you to reposition the flowers, pulling them up higher or down lower if needs be.

step 4

Continue adding your flowers at a slight diagonal in a varied order, trying to avoid two of the same flowers sitting too close together. Each time you add a few stems turn the bunch using your free hand so that you are conscious of what is happening at every angle. Keep all stems facing in the same direction. As they are added, the twist will become obvious.

step 5

Stop when you are happy with the shape and size of your arrangement – bearing in mind the size of the jar. Hold the flowers in front of the vessel so you can measure how much of the stems to cut off. It is always better to be on the safe side and cut your stems a little longer than they need be, so you have the option to make them shorter.

step 6

Place the arrangement into the jar, letting the flowers fall naturally. You can now fiddle with the shape, adding or removing flowers as you see fit.

Turn over for examples of flowery filled jars and bottles.

K · 131

Kit

There are hundreds of things out there on the floristry market that you could buy to make the perfect floral arrangement. Here are our essentials (so essential that we keep an extra set of each in our van) but you can tailor this list to suit your own needs. (See stockist list at back of book.)

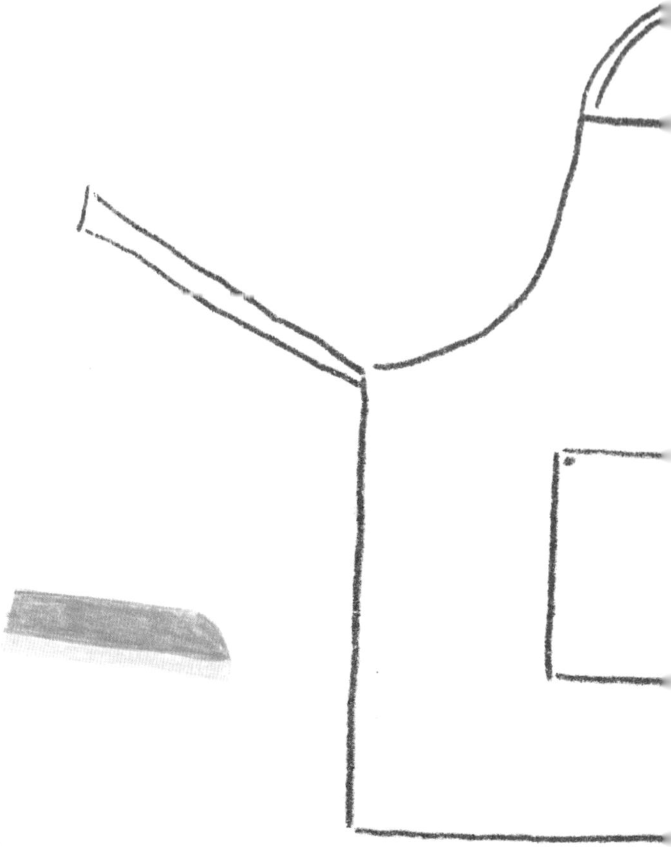

Knife

Apron

Water Spray

Bucket

Floristry Tape

Sticks of Thin Wire

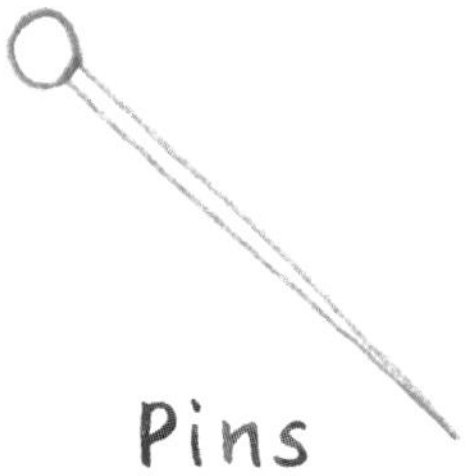

Pins

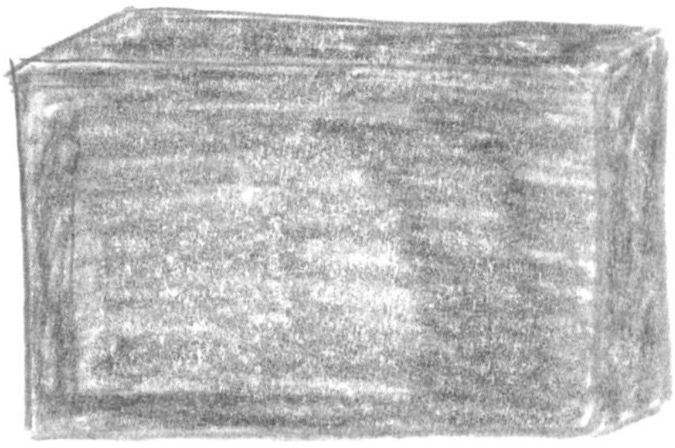

Floristry Foam

Floristry Scissors

Twine

Apron
Make sure it has good deep pockets!

A small sharp knife
Useful for de-thorning, cutting string and twine and slicing through blocks of floristry foam.

Floristry scissors
It's really worth investing in proper floristry scissors (they usually have yellow or orange handles). These are very sharp and cut through hard woody stems with ease, so be sure to handle with care! If you can't get hold of these, sharp household scissors or secateurs will do the job.

A selection of different width floristry wire
Vital for wiring individual flowers. Also essential when making our earrings, headdresses and individually wired hair flowers.

Floristry foam (Oasis)
You can buy this miracle stuff in bricks, large flat sheets and an array of shapes including every letter of the alphabet, hearts, shamrocks and much more. Before using it, the foam must be soaked in water. Brilliant when needing to place flowers in specific positions – we use it for our large arrangements, swan vases and white ceramic vases, see pages 238–242.

Buckets
If you are buying flowers in bulk it is a good idea to have a selection of different-sized buckets to hand to accommodate the variety of lengths that flowers come in. Short and squat for hydrangeas, sweet peas and dahlias. Tall, supportive containers for flowers like delphiniums, larkspur and peonies. And large wide buckets for bushy foliage.

Twine
It looks like string, but has a flexible wire vein making it wonderfully bendy and tough. We use this every day, especially for tying bouquets – both hand-tied and bridal, you don't need too much, 10cm will do. Wrap it around your bunch once, securing with a twist.

Floristry tape (Stemtex)
This sticky and stretchy tape is a godsend when making headdresses. (See pages 102–3.)

Water sprayer
A must on a hot day. We spray our flowers and occasionally ourselves when everything is a bit too hot and sticky. Also useful when the flowers you are using have to be out of water for long periods of time or sat in Oasis where their water supply is more limited.

Pins
Essential for buttonholes and finishing off the ribbon on bridal bouquets (see pages 30–3).

Lily-of-the-Valley

SEASON: APRIL–MAY

An all time favourite for its sweet and delicate fragrance, we love adding lily-of-the-valley (*Convallaria*) to bridal bouquets, bridesmaid bouquets and all sorts of small arrangements. It has little bonnet-like white flowers which climb the top of the stem and big green leaves. Add them to your arrangements at the last minute as they don't last long. They are by far the smallest flowers that we buy at the market, so small that we keep them in jam jars rather than buckets before using them. Highly poisonous if eaten, lily-of-the-valley is also known as Our Lady's tears and May bell and is part of the lily (*Liliaceae*) family.

Lilac

SEASON: MAY–JUNE

Belonging to the *Oleaceae* (olive) family, lilac (*Syringa vulgaris*) has a relatively short season. There is a clear difference between home-grown lilac (which we buy by the bunch from our English foliage supplier) and the lilac which is especially cultivated and imported from overseas. Gloriously scented British lilac has windy, nobbly stems, making it slightly harder to use and dictating the vase it can sit in. Cultivated lilac is grown with extraordinarily straight stems making it more user friendly but takes away a little of its character. It also has a less noticeable smell.

The sweet delicate scent, the soft full shape (which works particularly well in large arrangements) and the colours, are just a few reasons why we get excited every time lilac pops up at the market. Not only is there 'lilac'-coloured lilac but also bright white, rich purple, deep cerise and rose-tinted blush.

Watch out though, it is prone to wilting. To help it stay strong and happy, slit up the woody stem, maximising its drinking area (see page 55).

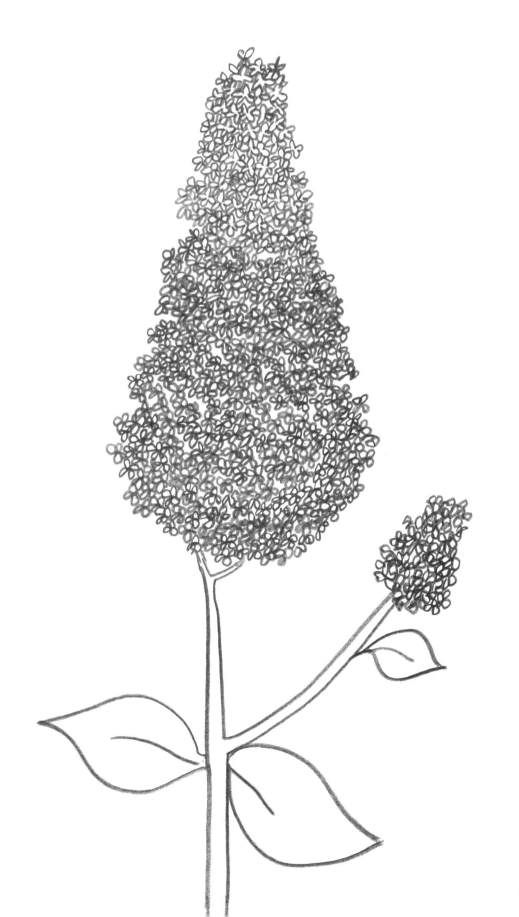

Large Pot

We bought this pair of simple white pots at Wimbledon car-boot sale when we first started. Little did we know how useful they would be. They are solid and sturdy, which is just what you need when making very large displays. We always use floristry foam in these pots as this allows us to place the flowers where we want them to sit.

If you want to make a large arrangement consider your container carefully – the wider the neck the better as you can fit more flowers in it. If you want to go really tall we recommend using opaque glass or ceramic vases so you can hide the foam in the vase. It will then act as a building block, allowing you to use different length stems in your arrangement.

Love-in-a-Mist

SEASON: JULY–SEPTEMBER

Named thanks to its fennel-like fronds (the 'mist') surrounding the delicate flower (the 'love'), this unassuming little flower, properly known as *Nigella damascene*, is also sometimes called 'devil in a bush' and, to the great amusement of the boys at the market, 'shag in the dark'. It is a member of the buttercup family.

It is available in white, raspberry, cornflower and sky blue. We like to remove the wispy leaves from up and down the stem. Sometimes, when the 'mist' is particularly thick, we remove some of that as well to reveal more of the flower. The stems are easily broken so handle with care. Great for jam jars and cut glass.

Lupins

SEASON: MAY–JULY

Its name derives from the Latin word for wolf – *Lupus* – but it reminds us more of the bright plumage on an exotic bird. Another short-seasoned flower, we are thrilled to see lupins (*Lupinus*) when they return to the market. We buy them in mixed rainbow-coloured buckets from our English supplier – lipstick pink, dark claret, lemon yellow, golden orange, royal purple and dusty lilac. These tropical coloured blooms from the *Leguminosae* family need to be in water at all times, otherwise their proud points will flop. They have a short but beautiful life span.

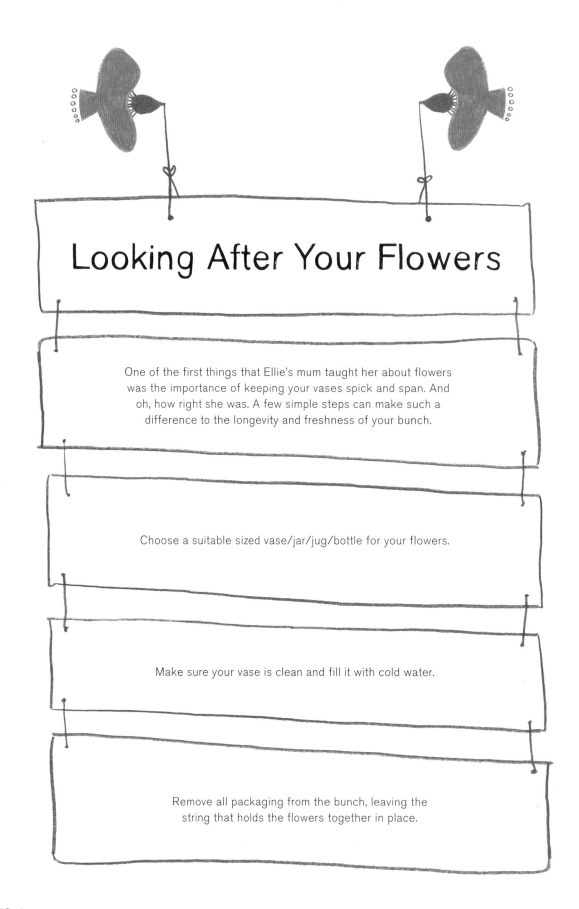

Looking After Your Flowers

One of the first things that Ellie's mum taught her about flowers was the importance of keeping your vases spick and span. And oh, how right she was. A few simple steps can make such a difference to the longevity and freshness of your bunch.

Choose a suitable sized vase/jar/jug/bottle for your flowers.

Make sure your vase is clean and fill it with cold water.

Remove all packaging from the bunch, leaving the string that holds the flowers together in place.

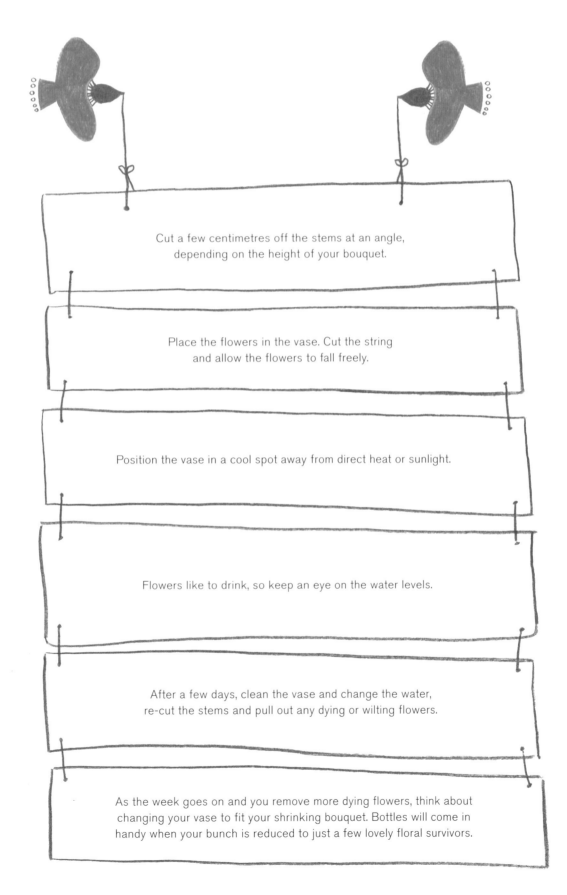

Cut a few centimetres off the stems at an angle,
depending on the height of your bouquet.

Place the flowers in the vase. Cut the string
and allow the flowers to fall freely.

Position the vase in a cool spot away from direct heat or sunlight.

Flowers like to drink, so keep an eye on the water levels.

After a few days, clean the vase and change the water,
re-cut the stems and pull out any dying or wilting flowers.

As the week goes on and you remove more dying flowers, think about
changing your vase to fit your shrinking bouquet. Bottles will come in
handy when your bunch is reduced to just a few lovely floral survivors.

Market

NOT YOUR AVERAGE MARKET

We buy our flowers at New Covent Garden market, London. We love it not just because it's the biggest flower, fruit and vegetable market in the UK, but also because of the fantastic atmosphere. Even on cold, rainy, dark winter mornings when it's a struggle getting out of bed, we still want to go because of the wonderful traders who are there to welcome us, the unique feeling of the place and its amazing history.

The market began over four hundred years ago in Covent Garden, selling fruit and vegetables, flowers and herbs. By the early nineteenth century the railways had opened up the country to fresh flowers, business was booming and a specialist flower market had to be built. A century later there were over 460 flower stalls selling entirely British produce, and in the mid 1970s the market outgrew its home in Covent Garden and moved to a new purpose-built site at Nine Elms, Vauxhall. Today our wonderful market faces serious competition from supermarkets and florists taking deliveries direct from Holland. There are fewer traders than there once were, but this does nothing to dampen the vibrant spirit of the place with its riot of colours and scents.

Here are the stories of some of the traders who work there:

Dennis

Wholesaler of the year, 'man of the year' (in his own words), Dennis has worked at the market for forty-eight years and is one of the longest running traders and the president of the tenants' association. He is a third-generation market seller and when he started he was at the old flower market. 'In the summer you had to sell it the same day or sling it. In the winter, everything froze. Stands were tiny, and because everything was British, pretty much the only flowers available were carnations, asparagus and chrysanthemum blooms.' His grandson is also called Dennis and his granddaughters are called Violet and Poppy (poppies also happen to be his favourite flowers). Statice is his least favourite flower.

Al

'It's in my blood,' says Al, who has been working at the market on and off for fifty years. His family have been in the trade since the late-nineteenth century. Today he works alongside his son Eddie and grandson Sonny, all three on the same stall. He has many strings to his bow, including doing a degree in his fifties, being a black cab driver and writing short stories for children. When he's not working at the market, he loves long-distance running. Forty miles in under five hours is his best achievement to date!

Edwin

Eddie has an incredible collection of hats (over 200) and a tattoo of a devil on his bum. Aged six, he began accompanying his dad (Al) to the Old Covent Garden market where he made tea for the traders, swept out their vans and cleaned the buckets. At fourteen he got his first job at New Covent Garden. 'I love work, I do it because I want to do it. The money comes extra.'

Eddie sleeps for two hours a day, loves shopping and his favourite flower is the trusty carnation. He met his wife, now a florist, on a coach to Zero 6 disco in Southend when she was sixteen and he was eighteen.

Sonny

After leaving performing-arts college, Sonny joined the family business on 3 September 2012 when he was twenty years old. 'I wasn't in to flowers at all,' he says. He started off sweeping, cleaning the dirty buckets and keeping the place tidy. Two months in and Sonny's real initiation took place. On a busy morning, a sales book was thrust into his hand and that's when the magic happened. He fell in love with the buzz of selling and there was no looking back. His favourite flower is the rose and he plays golf at least three times a week once his flowery day is over.

Richie

Richie helped his grandad on his flower stall at
Covent Garden market (which he had until he was
eighty-one!) when he was a young boy and got a job
at New Covent Garden market when he was sixteen.
'I love it here, I love the atmosphere, the people. It's
hard hours but I love it.' He met his wife at school and
they have been married for twenty-eight years. They
have three children. Richie loves football and boxing
– he boxed professionally from the ages of eleven to
twenty-four. His favourite flower is the dahlia (he is
the main supplier of English dahlias at the market)
and his least favourite flower is the tulip. 'I said to
Bobby, if ever I won the lottery I would order three
trolleys of tulips, put them on the floor and jump all
over them – that's how much I hate them! You come
in one day they're lovely and the next day . . . aaaah!'

Punchy

'It's been a pleasure; loved every day,' says Punchy.
A career lasting thirty-five years and he still has the
same enthusiasm as he did on day one. At one point
Punchy and all three of his brothers were porters at
the market. In the eighties, Punchy was a professional
boxer (hence his name) and his favourite place to fight
was the Royal Albert Hall. He gave it up because he's
a 'performer not a fighter'. He recently married his
partner of twenty-seven years in Las Vegas and most
weeks he takes flowers home to her.

Maurice

When Maurice first started working at the flower market thirty years ago, more than twenty members of his family including his brother, two brothers-in-law, fifteen cousins, a couple of uncles and his dad all worked there too. It was spring and Maurice remembers that the smell was unbelievable – the daffs, the freesias . . . 'You could get high on the smell of mimosa alone.' Packed with boxes of English flowers as high as the ceiling, 'everyone swearing and effing and blinding; people coming in drunk, women dancing, film stars walking about'.

For Maurice, working at the market has been the best job ever; he loves the camaraderie. When he retires he'll buy a boat, stick it at the end of his garden and fish all day long. He loves donkeys, gorillas and dogs.

Saul

Saul started working at the market when he was seventeen. 'My old man Bob works on the same firm, I just sort of fell into it. It goes back generations in my family.' He loves working at the market but hates the hours – he gets up between 10 p.m. and 1.30 a.m. depending on what day of the week it is. To relax, Saul likes to make music and add to his ever-growing collection of trainers.

Charlie

Charlie is Adil's cousin and came to help last Christmas when GB Foliage were short staffed. He writes in his spare time: the Tudors and pre-Imperial Rome are his specialities. Charlie loves ancient history, tattoos (he's got 'between forty and fifty'!) composing classical music and playing in his heavy metal band. His favourite foliage is mimosa.

Dave

Dave got his first job working on a foliage stand twenty-six years ago and started up his own business, GB Foliage, five years ago. His dad was a greengrocer, so early mornings and customer service are in his blood, 'service costs nothing' he says. The foliage which is available today has changed a great deal, 'Back in the day, all you could get was pine, moss and asparagus fern'. Dave's favourite foliage is stephanandra because it's a lovely colour, it flows and isn't too rigid – he likes a wilder style of floristry.

When he's not working you can find Dave at his allotment; he loves growing vegetables. He's passionate about steam engines and horse racing.

Adil

Adil spotted a job advert on Gumtree six years ago and has been working for Dave ever since. Work starts at 1 a.m. on a Monday morning, but he doesn't mind the hours because he's a nighttime person. He will stay working at the market as long as Dave stays. When he's not working, he loves gardening, cooking, horse riding and visiting his family in Morocco. Adil's favourite foliage is mint.

Zak

Zak got a job working for Dave at GB Foliage when he was eighteen, four years ago. He likes the vibe at the market: 'you don't really get it anywhere else. It's so laid back.' Zak's favourite foliage is variegated privet and his top flower is the hydrangea.

Mother's Day Bouquet

HOW TO MAKE A HAND-TIED BOUQUET

Mother's Day falls in spring and is one of the first signs that the long winter months are behind us. Follow the simple steps below to make your mum her own beautiful homemade bouquet, much more special than buying one ready made.

You Will Need:

Twine, scissors, 2 x pieces of A2 paper, sellotape.

Flowers We Have Used:

Delphiniums, phlox, *Hydrangea paniculata*, cosmos, Japanese anemone, dahlia, roses, dill, lysimachia and weigela.

step 1

Fill a bucket with a selection of different sized and shaped flowers, fillers and foliage. Let them have a good drink and condition them (see pages 54–5).

Arrange the flowers, fillers and foliage into neat groups on the table in front of you.

step 2

Choose a leading flower (here we have used a delphinium) and hold it in your left hand (the reverse if you are left-handed).

step 3

Next select a different colour and shape flower and sit it on top of the first so that the stems diagonally overlap each other.

step 4

Continue adding your flowers in this way, choosing different flowers each time to keep the bunch looking varied. Each time you add a few stems turn the bouquet using your free hand so that you are conscious of what is happening at every angle. The stems will naturally form a twist and start to 'spiral'. Place any fragile, soft-stemmed flowers like tulips, anemone and ranunculus in the middle of the bunch so they are supported by the hardier stems around them.

step 5

When you are happy with the size of your bouquet add a nice mix of different foliage around the outside and twist a piece of twine around the stems to secure them. At this point it is good to pull up any flowers which have slipped down and got lost in the bouquet. Make sure you do this very carefully though, as it's easy to snap their heads off!

step 6

Cut the stems so that the bouquet measures about 50cm.

step 7

Take two pieces of A2 wrapping paper (we use white and buy it in big packs from the market), hold the first sheet at opposite corners, folding in half to make two points. Repeat this with the second piece of paper.

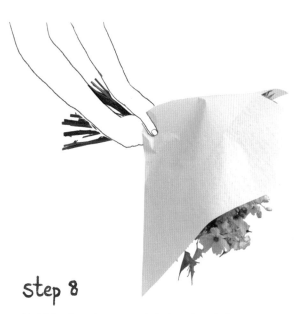

step 8

Hold the bunch in your right hand and place one piece of paper on top of the flowers, pinching the paper slightly where your hand is. Turn your hand the other way up, facing the bouquet to the floor. Neatly pull the two corners of the paper together and sellotape to secure.

step 9

Take the second piece of paper and place it so that its points fill in the gaps which the other paper has left. You should have six points in all. Sellotape to join the edges together.

step 10

Once your bouquet is wrapped, again it's good to carefully pull up any flowers which have fallen down into the bouquet and loosen it up a little so it doesn't look too tight.

YOUR
RAGE
STS

HOW WE BEGAN...

Anna Day

I finished a degree in illustration in 2005. I had a few wandering years post-university which took me everywhere from dog walking in Barcelona to teaching in Shanghai. Finally I settled back in London, around the corner from where I grew up and my parents still live. I embarked on a career in illustration, but the solitary days spent drawing and looking for work took their toll and I wanted to add a new string to my bow. I decided to enrol on a year-long floristry course and found myself working behind a bar in my local pub for extra money . . .

Ellie Jauncey

Growing up in rural Herefordshire, I always knew I wanted to live in London and so with a textile degree and love of all things knitted, I made the move to the big smoke in 2006. I tried various jobs in the fashion and textile world, but after a few years when I was still searching for the dream job I ended up spending a summer helping my mother (also a florist) with lots of weddings back home in Herefordshire. On my return to London, I decided I wanted to give floristry a go and so I got work experience in a florists and a job in a local pub to help make ends meet . . .

Anna and Ellie

So this is how we met, working behind the bar of The Scoll Head Pub in Hackney. Many a night spent pouring pints together led to flowery chats and we realised how much we had in common. Very slowly but surely, the seeds for The Flower Appreciation Society were sown.

First of all we started making weekly arrangements for the pub – it brightened up the place no end. We saved the money we earned from making these weekly flowers so that we could buy a camera. Then we started taking photos of our creations and building a portfolio.

Word started to spread and a few weddings came our way. At this point we didn't have a studio or any money, so had to be resourceful. We often ended up working from the kitchen table in one of our houses. For bigger jobs we pleaded with our boss (and great friend) Rosie to let us use the pub's function room and on a sunny day you could find us beavering away in the car park. Storage inevitably became an issue and after a while we took over the shed at the pub, filling it with boxes of vases, jars and bottles. To this day we are indebted to Rosie for allowing us to use the pub in this way. Another crucial ingredient to these humble beginnings was our Toyota Previa. Having been Anna's family car for years, it now became our trusty flower transporter. Covered in dents and cracks (some even held together with gaffer tape) and with a temperamental heating system, we certainly didn't look the part, but it did the job.

Now we needed a name . . . We didn't realise how hard this would be. An early suggestion was 'Jauncey & Day', which we both agreed sounded more like a solicitor's than a florist. Back in the pub one evening, and with the help of our wonderful co-worker Chris, we finally got there. Our favourite Neil Young album was playing in the background and Chris said, 'How about calling your florist The Neil Young Appreciation Society?!' And Anna replied, 'No, it's got to be The Flower Appreciation Society!' As soon as she said it, we knew we'd got it.

Next on the list was designing our website. Anna played around with drawing, collaging, using old photos and handwriting. She was pleased that she could put her illustration background to such good use, and slowly but surely our identity started to take shape. Having a website changed everything. We now had a proper platform to promote ourselves. →

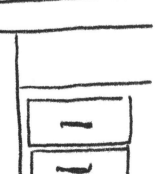

This ad-hoc way of working was fine for two years, but eventually the shed began to overflow and the Previa started making strange noises. It was time for The Flower Appreciation Society to grow up. We bought a van and found a studio.

Four years on, we continue to work from our studio in De Beauvoir, London. We share the space with three other creative friends. The walls are lined with shelves housing our ever-growing collection of vases and vessels and there is a large communal table in the middle of the room where we hold our flowery workshops. We like the freedom of having a studio rather than a shop; it means we never throw flowers away as we buy to order. With weddings every weekend, events and classes throughout the week, there is never a dull moment. We love what we do.

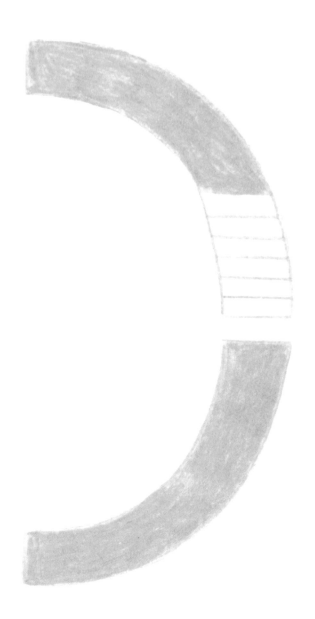

Our Colourful Crates

Colour, colour, colour! It's all about colour!

When delivering our flowers, we pack them tightly into plastic vegetable crates, which shows off their colours brilliantly. Here are some of our favourite flowery crates for some colour-combination inspiration . . .

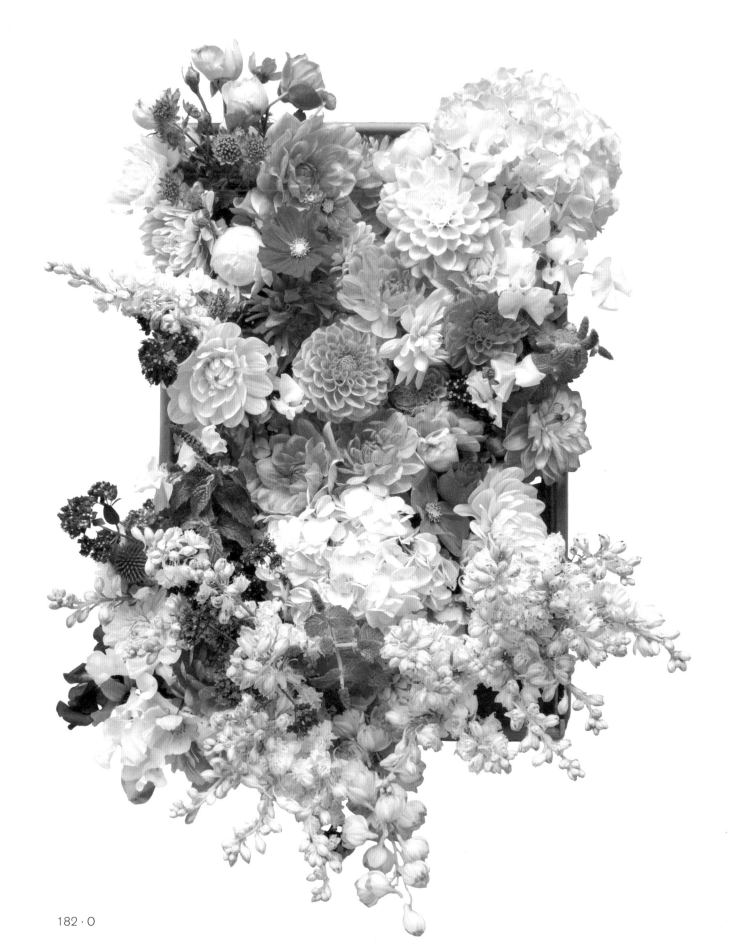

Peony

SEASON: MAY–JULY

Definitely the most popular flower on our shopping list – almost everyone loves a peony (from the *Paeonia* family). From single layered petals (exposing glowing yellow stamens) to fluffy balls of multi-layered petals, there is a different variety of peony for everyone. At the height of their season, the market has a wonderful array of colours: white, very pale blush, light pink, shocking pink, coral, magenta and a rather random acid yellow. Beware, these blooms open extremely quickly so buy in bud if you need them to last. The only sad thing about these beauties is the slightly fishy smell which sometimes develops with age. But don't be put off, their glory definitely overrides their odour. They work brilliantly in almost all arrangements, adding drama and luxury. Or for a simple way to use these magnificent flowers, try putting a bunch of open blooms in a big jar or a single stem in a bottle.

A Magical Peony

A DAY IN THE LIFE OF A CORAL CHARM PEONY

Twelve hours is all it takes for this magical flower to transform from shocking cerise to bright coral to a faded bleached-out pink. What a difference a day makes!

9am

2pm

7pm

Pickle Jars

We discovered the wonder of the pickle jar while working at the pub down the road, where the locals love a burger with the obligatory gherkin. The gherkins are delivered to the kitchen in generous sized jars (just over 20cm tall) – the 'pickle jar'. Not only are they great for medium-sized arrangements, they are also a perfect vessel for delivering our bridal bouquets in. To this day, the lovely chefs at the pub keep them for us in the cellar to collect once a week.

Poppy

SEASON: JUNE–AUGUST

One day, driving back from a big job in Norfolk, we happened to pass fields full of rows and rows of poppies either side of the road, creating a glowing red blanket. We jumped out of the van and danced around the poppies, filled with joy. This is where our huge appreciation of the poppy began. Apart from their signature poppy red, they also come in glorious sunset shades. These wondrous colours are revealed once the strange, hairy, outside sepals which encase the fragile papery petals begin to open. We buy Icelandic poppies from the market which are hardier than their field poppy relatives. They're lovely in bouquets and all sized arrangements, but tricky to use in floristry foam as the stems are bendy and soft. Handle with care! Poppies are part of the *Papaveraceae* family.

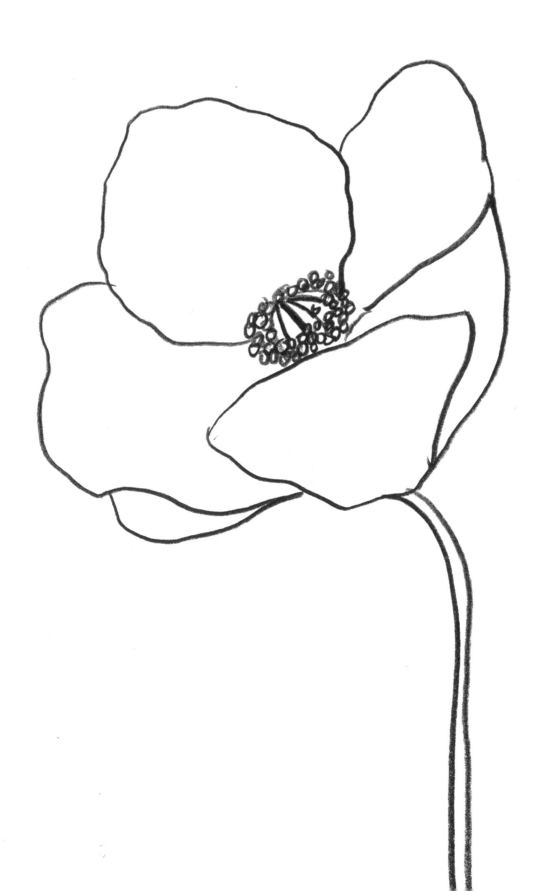

Queen Bee
and Her Subjects

When the studio is full of flowers and the doors are flung open, we often have little buzzing bee visitors. We are reminded that flowers are not simply just for our pleasure. They serve a real purpose.

Bees are under threat due to insecticides, the loss of their natural habitat and diseases. We can all help by planting bee-friendly flowers in our gardens and window boxes. You can buy wildflower seed mixes, or choose specific flowers to plant. They particularly like simple, single flowers such as scabious, cosmos and dahlias but are not so keen on densely petalled flowers as it is harder for them to get to the nectar. They love anything purple, blue or yellow as these are the colours they can see the best, so try planting lavender, aquilegia or cornflowers to attract bees into your garden. They are also attracted to tubular-shaped flowers like foxgloves and snapdragons. It was vital to include these hard workers in our book. Without them there would be no flowers at all.

This is how the queen bee's dutiful subjects pollinate flowers . . .

pollen grains

While eating the sugary nectar, which is made by the flowers at the base of the pistil, some of the pollen rubs onto the bee's back from the anthers.

brightly coloured petals

Bees are attracted to bright colours and lovely sweet-smelling flowers.

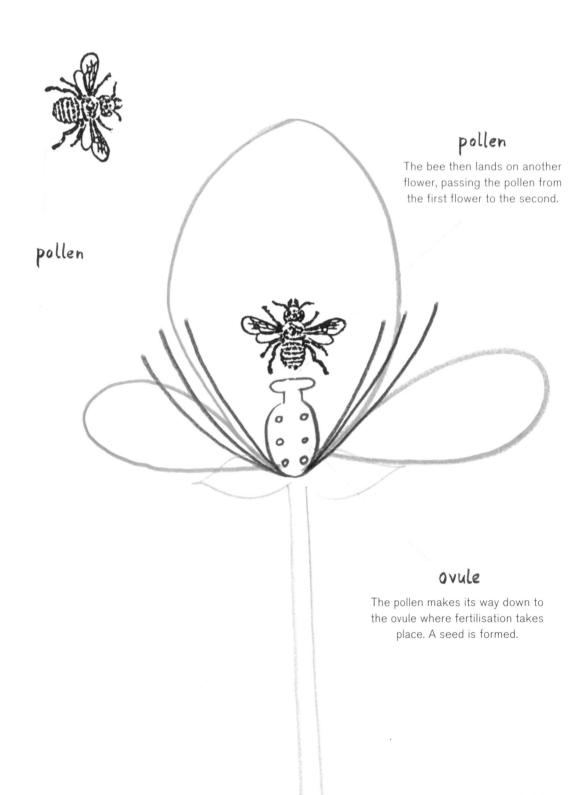

pollen

pollen

The bee then lands on another flower, passing the pollen from the first flower to the second.

ovule

The pollen makes its way down to the ovule where fertilisation takes place. A seed is formed.

Ranunculus

SEASON: APRIL

The name *Ranunculus* comes from the Latin word for little frog – 'Rana' – and is part of the Buttercup family.

There are many different varieties of *Ranunculus*, the most commonly available to buy being the *Ranunculus asiaticus*. When closed, these resemble tight, spherical pom-poms, slowly opening to reveal layer upon layer of fine petals in a complex structure. Like the peony and some roses, once fully opened (which can take over a week) this lovely flower looks completely different from its budded origins. Petals that were once tightly packed have now relaxed, and are airy and light so that their colour can be displayed in all their glory. These early spring treats come in a marvellous paint box of colours: snowy white, chalky pink, sharp yellow, ochre, warm orange, hot pink, flaming red, rich plum, deep violet and an almost black oxblood. Look out for pale coloured *Ranunculas* that look like they've had the petal edges dipped in pink, red or purple dye.

Ranunculus have fragile stems and are easily snapped, so be careful when using them.

Rose

SEASON: JUNE–OCTOBER

More poems have been written about the rose (*Rosa*) than any other flower. We use this versatile bloom in almost everything we make: buttonholes, headdresses, bouquets, confetti and many of our arrangements. There are hundreds of different varieties available – look at rose specialist David Austin's website to get an idea of the choice that is out there. He sells over 800 varieties of roses, both cut and planted. As well as the rose itself, plums, pears, cherries, apricots, apples and peaches all belong to the *Rosaceae* family.

Unbelievably, roses are available at the market all year round in a wealth of shapes and colours, as many are grown in exotic climes. In the summer months, try buying their delightful British counterparts which often have a sweeter, stronger fragrance and a wonderful delicate charm.

We are naturally drawn to the soft, blowsy, old English-style rose, but the neater, more structured varieties such as the Norma Jean or Avalanche are also readily available. Spray roses, with their multiple branches, have several small flowers per stem and are invaluable when making buttonholes and bridal headdresses.

The amount of thorns on a stem varies hugely from rose to rose. Some are so densely covered it's hard to see the stem at all, whereas others have only a few spikes. Some are sharp like daggers and others much gentler, with soft curved tips. Be extra careful when dealing with these vicious little beauties – you might want to wear gardening gloves.

R · 205

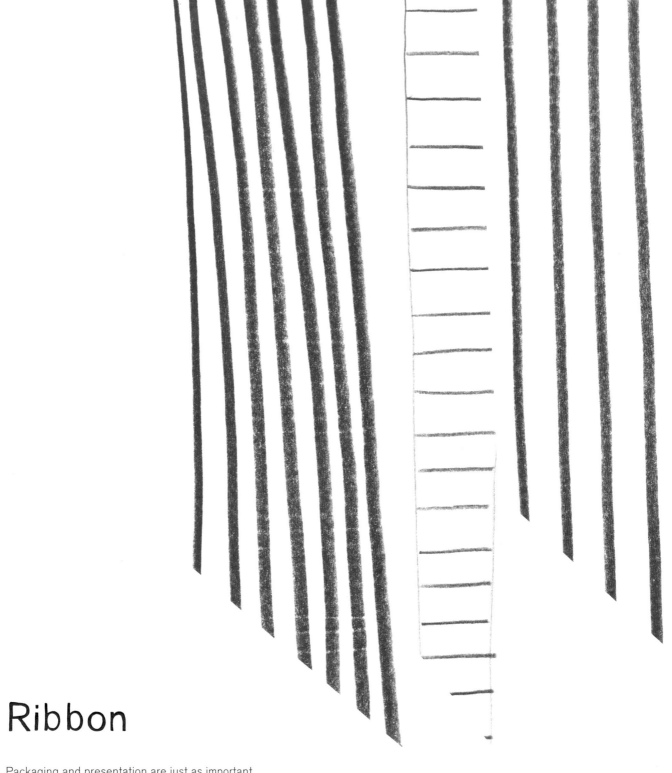

Ribbon

Packaging and presentation are just as important
to us as the flowers themselves, but you do not
need expensive materials. We use simple, plain
white paper and a beautiful ribbon: try grosgrain,
striped or block colour and tie with a big bow.

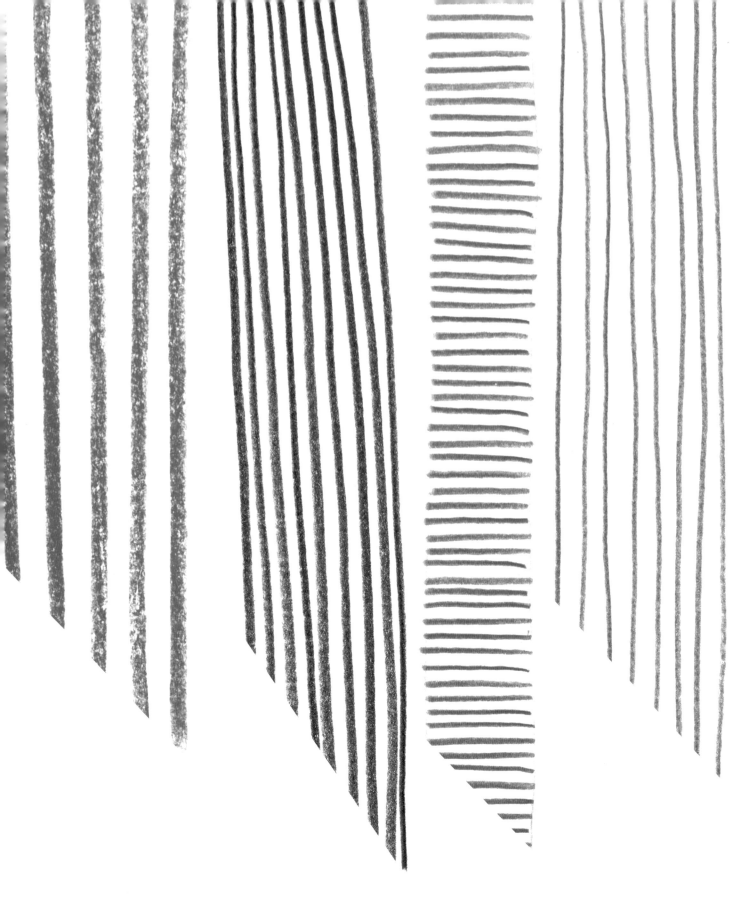

R · 207

Stocks

SEASON: APRIL–OCTOBER

With their strong clove scent and full petals, stocks (*Matthiola*) make wonderful fillers and are great at padding out any arrangement. They have sturdy stems so work especially well in floristry foam. Available in pastel pink, nude, vanilla, shiny white, soft lilac, shocking pink and deep purple, they are a part of the *Cruciferae* family. Sometimes the tips of their heads can be a little scraggly and seem thinner than the rest of the flower. If this is the case, chop off this top section at the point where the flowers start to become dense, leaving you with only the full-flowering section remaining.

Swans

COLOUR AND FLOWER INSPIRATION

Scent

Flowers have a scent to entice insects to pollinate them, but they also attract humans. Our top five perfumed favourites are: roses, sweet peas, lilac, lavender and mint. Other lovely fragrant flowers are: stocks, lily-of-the-valley, chocolate cosmos (it really smells of chocolate!), hyacinths, camille, oregano, dill, rosemary, eucalyptus, wax flower, philadelphus and jasmine.

We tend to avoid certain flowers such as freesias and lilies which have very strong scents. We definitely prefer a subtler, softer smell to an intense perfume. We've noticed that when we buy British blooms, their scents are stronger than their imported relatives and have often wondered why. Gill Hodgson from Flowers from the Farm explained it to us: flowers that are imported from distant lands such as South America and Africa have to spend days travelling without much water so they are cultivated to have strong straight stems, hardy blooms and a long-lasting shelf life rather than a sweet-smelling fragrance. Flowers will still sell without a scent.

The same demands are not made on British flowers because they're more likely to come from a field down the road than hundreds of miles away, and are grown on a much smaller scale. Another great reason to buy British!

Sweet Pea

SEASON: MAY – SEPTEMBER

Like the peony, this is a very popular flower and one of our all-time favourites. Available in every colour under the sun apart from yellow (although sweet pea breeders are on a quest to make this happen), the season never feels quite long enough. If only this page was scratch and sniff so that you could smell their lovely scent. Sweet peas (*Lathyrus odoratus*) have relatively short stems, and look just as good on their own in a vase as they do mixed in with other flowers.

In early summer, at the height of the wedding season, we buy mixed bunches in large boxes. Lying in their cardboard bed, protected by a blanket of tissue paper, it is always a joy to open the lid to see and smell our flowery treasure.

Occasionally we spot the everlasting sweet pea, which have smaller fuchsia flowers and tangly stems (look out for these winding round bushes, trees and garden gates). We buy these at the market, still on their vines, rather than as cut flowers – they look wonderful in large arrangements, tumbling out of the sides of the vessel.

S·217

Scabious

SEASON: JUNE–OCTOBER

One of the delights that the summer brings is the paper-thin, delicate scabious (*Caucasica*), which comes in crisp white, icy blue, the palest of lilacs and royal blue. For such a pretty flower, it really does have a very ugly name! It comes from the word 'scabies' – the itching disease that this little flower was said to cure. Another rather more attractive name for them is the 'pin-cushion' flower. We use these in big and small arrangements alike.

S · 219

Tulips

SEASON: APRIL–MAY

Originating in Ottoman Turkey, the tulip (*Tulipa*) has a rich and dramatic history. There are whole books dedicated to this flower. Anna Pavord's *The Tulip* is a detailed chronicle of the trials and tribulations of this extraordinary flower. At the peak of its hype in seventeenth-century Holland, one rare tulip bulb was worth the same as an entire house. Today, the Dutch produce over four billion tulip bulbs a year. It appears that the hype is not over yet!

Found in the *Lilaceae* (lily) family, the varieties of tulip seem endless. From the primary-coloured common tulip to the flamboyant, frilly-edged wonders which can be found in the paintings of the old Dutch masters, the choice is overwhelming.

Tulips have very little scent but more than make up for this with their exquisite patterns, textures and colours; fabric-like fringes lining the edges of the petals, to dark contrasting colours making star formations at the base of the flower, blotches splattered, stripes intricately painted, edges dipped . . . this unbelievable spectrum of colours and form never ceases to astonish us.

Some tulips have a tendency to lean and bow, weighed down by their heavy heads, which makes them tricky to use in bouquets and arrangements. To help prevent this from happening, keep them wrapped in paper until you use them. Like the anemone they continue growing after they've been cut, so it's a good idea to trim them a little shorter than your other flowers.

Last spring Ellie visited Tammy, a flower grower in Herefordshire whose tulip fields were in full bloom. Neat rows of majestic tulips covered the ground in every imaginable colour. Ellie filled a bucket with the most sensational tulips she had ever seen – some as big as Easter eggs and others with a surprising, sweet fragrance. Turn over to see these glorious flowers . . .

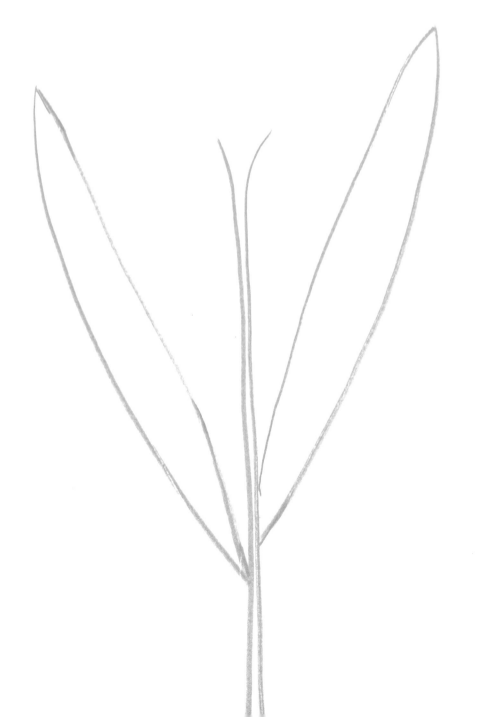

T · 223

Urn

Our urn vases are the ideal size for creating a medium to large display with lots of impact. Their lovely fanned-out shape works brilliantly sitting on window sills, on mantelpieces or on top of a plinth. Look out for them in charity shops and at car-boot sales.

The key to a beautiful urn arrangement is using a mixture of lots of different flowers and thinking about the shape throughout the making process. We always use blocks of floristry foam to build our urn arrangements (see pages 132–3 for tips on Kit). It's vital that the foam fits snugly in the container (by either trimming a block down or adding an extra piece) to give a really strong anchor to the display.

You Will Need:

Floristry foam, scissors and a clean urn.

Flowers We Have Used:

Delphiniums, hydrangeas, dahlias, cosmos, stocks, roses, sweet peas, astrantia, mint, beech and weigela.

step 1

Choose a suitable urn and a selection of flowers – tall, large, medium and small blooms – assorted foliage and plenty of fillers. Fill a bucket up with water and soak an appropriate amount of floristry foam for your container. Once it sinks to the bottom it is ready to use. (It will be heavy with water and the colour will have changed to very dark green.)

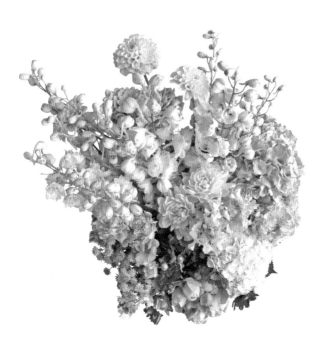

step 2

It is important to decide how tall you'd like the arrangement to be – about 70cm is a good height for a large urn. We then start with foliage. Choose a nice tall piece to become the central, highest part of the arrangement and put it in the middle of the foam. Keep adding the foliage either side of this central piece until you have created a fan shape. Make sure you place the stems at the back of the foam so that there is plenty of room for the flowers to sit in front.

step 3

Now add the tall flowers, making sure they are spaced out nicely and don't look too regularly placed. We have used delphiniums.

step 4

The larger blooms like hydrangeas and dahlias should be added next. Try to add the flowers randomly and push some stems further into the foam than others to create depth in your arrangement.

step 5

Now add the medium-sized flowers, again dotting them around – avoiding anything too neat or ordered. Here we have added cosmos, stocks and roses. At this point it's really helpful to stand back and look at the arrangement to see how the shape is looking.

step 6

Fillers, herbs and small flowers are next (sweet peas, mint and astrantia). Once these are all in, check to see where there are gaps and fill these in with whichever flowers you think will work best. Turn over for a few pages of our favourite flower-filled urns.

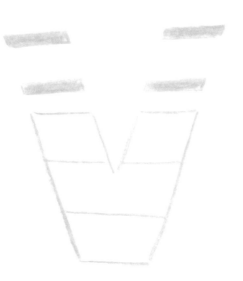

Vessels

The vessels we use are as important as the flowers we put in to them. Over the last four years we have scoured the country's charity shops, junk shops and car-boot sales to find vases of all shapes, sizes and designs. It is definitely one of the perks of our job and has become a bit of an addiction!

We have now built up a large collection which sits on the shelves above our desk in neat rows…

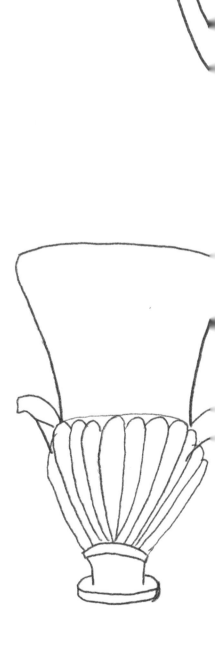

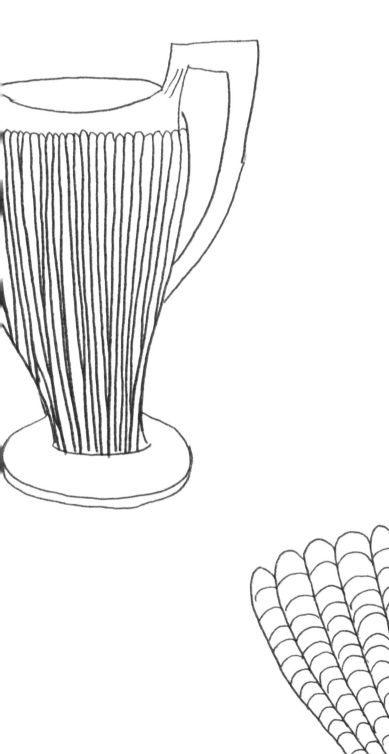

Jugs and White Ceramic Vases

We always look out for big old jugs, especially ones with great floral prints on them. At about 30cm tall, they are an incredibly useful size and the shape of the neck allows the flowers to fall in a lovely natural way.

We bought a job-lot of white vases at a car-boot sale about a year ago. We couldn't believe our luck when we rifled through a box and discovered the gems inside: upright shells, fish soap dishes, a whole family of ceramic trophy cups and a couple of our beloved white urns. Ever since we've been keeping our eye out and adding to the collection.

Urns

Urns are one of our favourite vessels to collect. Their low, wide-brimmed openings offer themselves to generous-sized arrangements as well as smaller, more compact, luxurious displays. The variety of pattern, shape and size which they come in and their art deco style makes them a joy to search for and use.

Swans

The old ceramic swans we have collected over the years are our pride and joy. Found at car-boot sales and junk shops, we are always on the look out for more to add to our forty-strong bevy. We have all different shapes and sizes. They make marvellous containers for both foam-based arrangements and hand-tied posies. A cheaper option, and also incredibly effective, is to fill the swan with a single big bloomed hydrangea head.

Cut-Glass Vases

The majority of old cut- or pressed-glass vases that you see today were made in the 1920s and 30s. Many were 'fairings' – cheap gifts you might win at the funfair. They come in a vast range of shapes and sizes with fantastically varied designs. Some are thick, some are thin, some terribly heavy, others rather light. We have over 150 in our collection and mostly use them for weddings.

White
Ceramic Vases

COLOUR AND FLOWER INSPIRATION

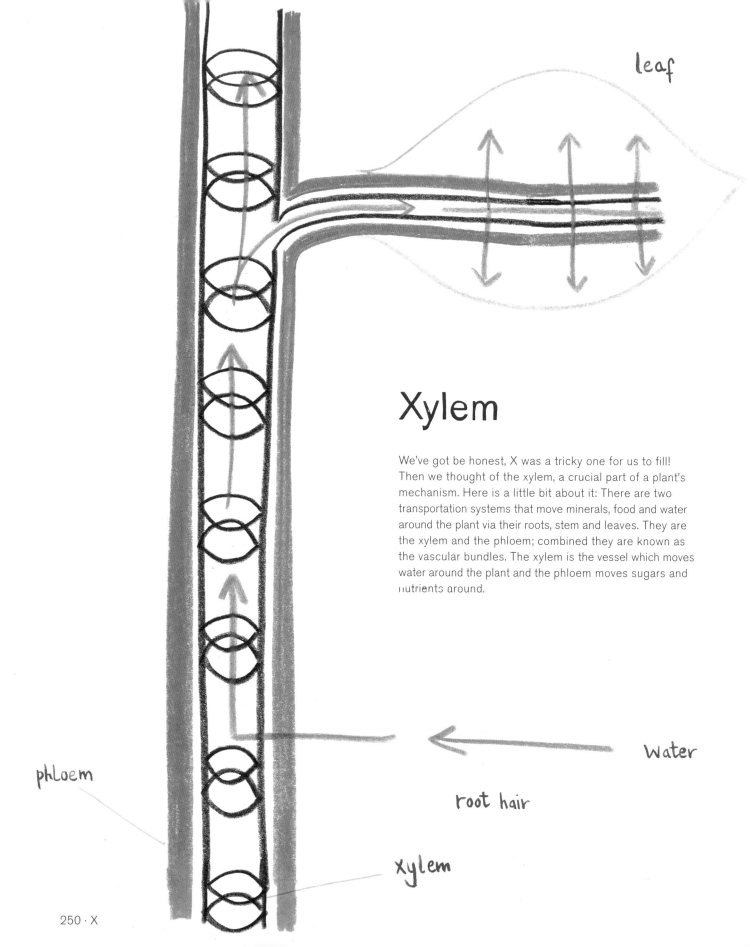

leaf

Xylem

We've got be honest, X was a tricky one for us to fill! Then we thought of the xylem, a crucial part of a plant's mechanism. Here is a little bit about it: There are two transportation systems that move minerals, food and water around the plant via their roots, stem and leaves. They are the xylem and the phloem; combined they are known as the vascular bundles. The xylem is the vessel which moves water around the plant and the phloem moves sugars and nutrients around.

Water

root hair

phloem

xylem

Cross-section of a stem

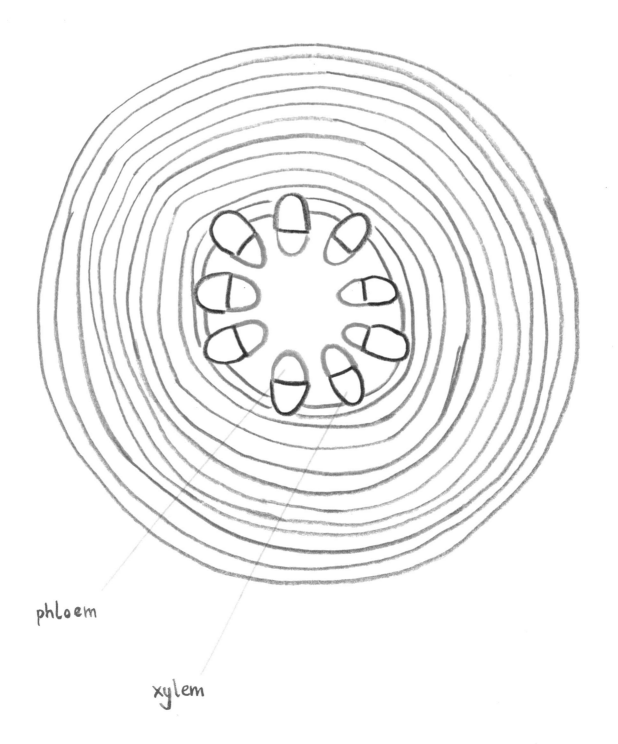

phloem

xylem

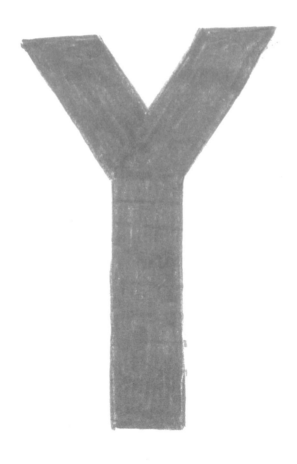

Y · 253

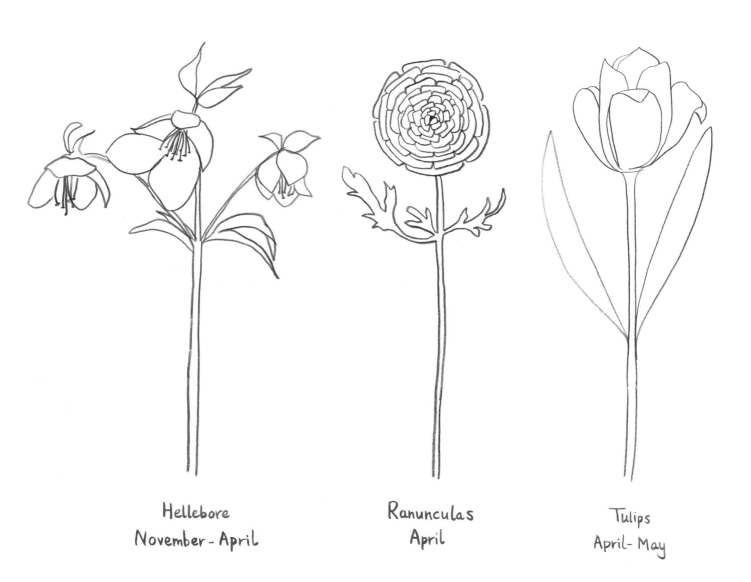

Hellebore
November - April

Ranunculas
April

Tulips
April - May

A Flowery Year

Here is a quick reference to the flowers we mention in the book, and when they are available. These are the British seasons rather than the imported flower seasons. Please bear in mind these seasons can vary slightly depending on the weather.

Anemone
April- May

Lily-of-the-Valley
April- May

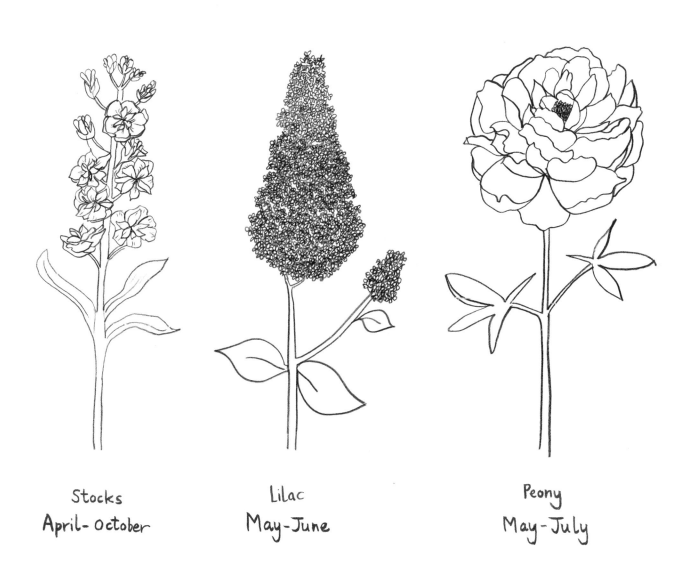

Stocks
April-October

Lilac
May-June

Peony
May-July

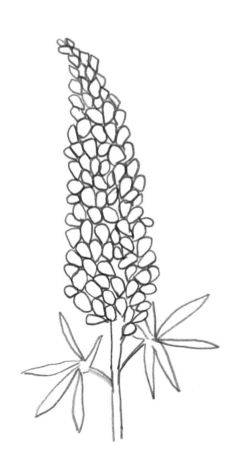

Lupins
May-July

Clematis
May- July

Ammi
May-August

Cornflower
May-August

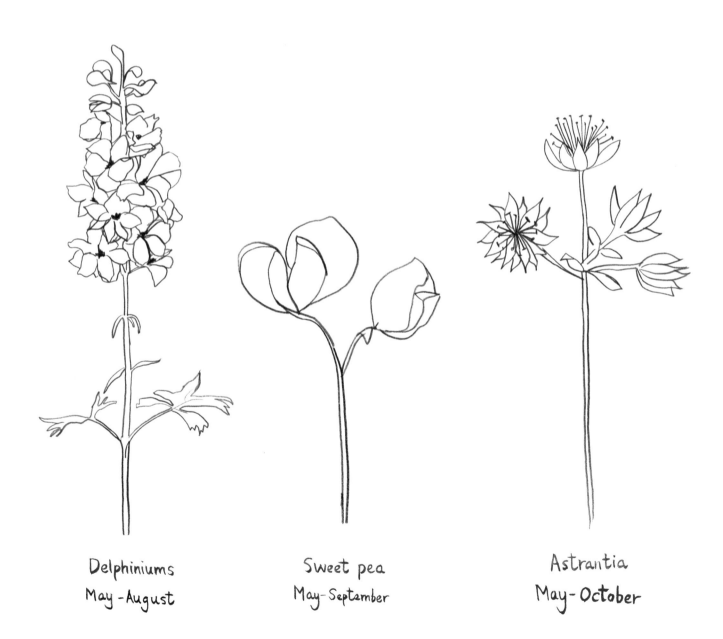

Delphiniums
May - August

Sweet pea
May - September

Astrantia
May - October

Aquilegia
June-July

Cosmos
June-September

Rose
June-October

Scabious
June-October

Hollyhock
July-August

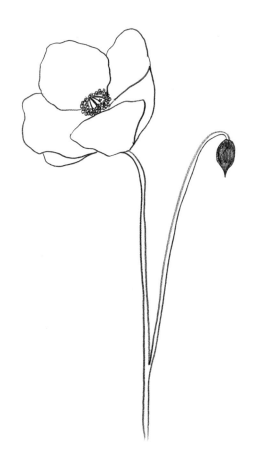

Poppy
June - August

Love-in-a-Mist
July - September

Zinnia
July - September

Dahlia
July - October

Hydrangea
July - November

Zinnia

SEASON: JULY–SEPTEMBER

These bright and hardy flowers are in the daisy family and were introduced from Mexico to Britain over 200 years ago. We adore their garish Indian colours of tangerine orange, mustard yellow, hot pink, paprika and dusky pink. They stand out from the crowd so we think they are best used on their own in a big bunch. Or try mixing them with another bold flower like the dahlia.

Z · 267

THE
END

Suppliers

New Covent Garden Market

These are just a few of our favourite traders at New Covent Garden Market.

FLOWERS:

Alagar Ltd: 020 7498 0170 / alagar@hotmail.co.uk

S. Robert Allen Ltd: 020 7720 9432

Bloomfield Wholesale Florist Ltd: 020 8444 0646
bloomfieldflowers@hotmail.co.uk

Dennis Edwards Flowers Ltd: 07956 378 685
sales@dennisedwardsflowers.com

D. G. Wholesale Flowers Ltd: 020 7738 8070
d.g_wholesaleflowers@hotmail.co.uk

A. Goodchild: 020 7720 7474
a.goodchild.ltd@btconnect.com
www.wholesale-florist.co.uk

Pratley Covent Garden Market Ltd: 020 7720 3914

Zest Flowers: 020 7498 7574 / zestflowers@gmail.com

FOLIAGE:

G. B. Foliage: 020 7720 1843

Porters: 020 7720 7831 / www.portersfoliage.com

SUNDRIES:

C. Best: 020 7720 2306 / www.cbest.co.uk

E. Pollard and Sons: 020 7720 6465

Whittingtons Ltd: 020 7720 9121

Other Flower Markets Nationwide

Birmingham: www.birminghamflowersandplants.co.uk

Bristol: www.flowervisionbristol.co.uk

Glasgow: www.jamestaylorflowers.com

Manchester: www.gbrflowers.co.uk

For other towns and cities have a look at
Van Vliet's website: www.jvanvliet.com

Online Sundries Suppliers

Florist foam: www.oasisfloral.co.uk

General supplies: www.sarahraven.com

Buying Direct from Holland

FleuraMetz: www.fleurametz.com

UK Flower Growers

The British Flower Collective:
www.thebritishflowercollective.com

Flowers from the Farm: www.flowersfromthefarm.co.uk

Tregothnan: www.tregothnan.co.uk/flowers-and-foliage

Specialist Rose Supplier

David Austin Roses: www.davidaustinroses.co.uk

Edible Flowers

Derek Lewis, First Leaf Flowers: www.firstleaf.co.uk

Bibliography

Complete Flower Arranging
Sheila Macqueen
Littlehampton Book Services, 1979

The Cutting Garden:
Growing and Arranging Garden Flowers
Sarah Raven
Frances Lincoln, 2013

English Gardens
Clive Nichols
The Land Gardeners Press, 2014

The Family of Flowers
Mea Allan, illustrated by Julia Morland
Pitman, 1979

Fifty Plants That Changed the Course of History
Bill Laws
David & Charles, 2010

Gardening Women:
Their Stories from 1600 to the Present
Catherine Horwood
Virago, 2010

Herbs (Classic Garden Plants)
Simon and Judith Hopkinson
Globe Pequot Press, 1989

The Illuminated Language of Flowers
Jean Marsh, illustrated by Kate Greenaway
Macdonald & J., 1978

Natural Companions:
The Garden Lover's Guide to Plant Combinations
Ken Druse
Stewart, Tabori & Chang Inc, 2012

The Oxford Book of Garden Flowers
E. B. Anderson, Margery Fish, A. P. Balfour,
Micheal Wallis, Valerie Finnis, B. E. Nicholson
Oxford University Press, 1963

Picturing Plants:
An Analytical History of Botanical Illustration
Gill Saunders
University of California Press, 1995

Pocket Encyclopaedia of Roses in Colour
Henry Edland
Blandford Press, 1963

RHS Botany for Gardeners:
The Art and Science of Gardening Explained and Explored
Geoff Hodge
Mitchell Beazley, 2013

Seven Flowers: and How They Shaped Our World
Jennifer Potter
Atlantic, 2013

The Tulip
Anna Pavord
Bloomsbury, 1999

Wild Flowers By Colour
Marjorie Blamey
Dorling Kindersley, 1997

Index

Appreciation

Rosie Wesemann – without you The Flower Appreciation Society would not exist.

Jackie Dalton for writing the rota around us for years.

The kitchen staff at the Scolt Head and Sylvester for the constant supply of pickle jars, crates and the odd sausage roll.

Emma Van Allan, our wonderfully generous website maker.

Freya Barlow and Hannah Speller for being our muses.

Thank you Dennis, Edwin, Al, Sonny, Dave, Adil, Zak, Charlie, Punchy, Richie, Maurice and Saul for letting us bombard you with questions for this book and making our early morning trips to the market such a joy.

Thank you to Edward and all in the Benyon office for providing the most wonderful studio for us to work in and to Bob the builder and his team for their fine carpentry skills.

The Seaton family for supporting us from the very start. Working with you made big things happen.

Ellie Pithers – thanks to you, the seed for this book was sown.

Ollie, Elliot, Ivan, Norman, Coco, Lisa, Amah-Rose, Alicia and Serge for letting us take over the upstairs studio day after day and always lending us your equipment.

Lizzie, Helen and Steph – thanks for being the best studio neighbours we could possibly have and for putting up with our weekly flower invasions.

Thank you to the inspirational Marie Murray and The Dalston Eastern Curve Garden for the joy you bring.

Rona Wheeldon for taking time to answer all of our flowery questions.

Gill Hodgson for promoting a cause that we believe in so strongly and for passing on your flower knowledge.

We can't thank Bridget Elworthy enough for being our go-to flower guru and inspiring us to be more green fingered.

Rivah – our beautiful headdress model, thank you for wearing it so well and trekking half way across London to get to us.

Eric, Simon and all at XY Digital for all those painstaking hours and hours . . . and hours of cutting out our flowers and everything else you've done for our book.

Hannah Speller and Maggie Colwell for spending your Christmas holiday trawling every page with a fine-tooth comb and giving us such thoughtful and constructive advice.

Emily Fox for your expert eye and an afternoon of great encouragement.

Isabel Crossman – thank God you came along, we couldn't have done this without you.

A massive thank you to all of our friends for believing in us from the start and spreading The Flower Appreciation Society word.

Thank you Will for showing us that you can mix business with pleasure. We appreciate the way you have made us look at things differently and your unbelievable patience (tested by the longest phone conversations ever). Thanks also to the other members of the Atwork team, Jen and Sam, for all your hard work with this book.

The Previa for never breaking down, even in extreme old age.

Thanks to Nick, Sian, Sarah and Stephie and all at Little, Brown for helping us to make this book. Thank you to Claudia Young for finding us and Hannah Boursnell for wanting us. Thanks to you both for making our dreams come true.

From Anna:

Thank you to my art teacher, Mr Jordan – Such an inspiring teacher who gave me such direct and brilliant advice when I was a lost eighteen year old.

Thank you to my mum and dad, Romee and Peter Day, for not only letting us use the family car for years whenever we wanted but for their unbelievable support for The Flower Appreciation Society. Benny Boy (a bit of an un-sung hero) and Issy for your ongoing generosity and help. Big sis Liz and THG (and Billy) for all those suppers and all that love. Jont and Nat (and Dora) for endless encouragement and PhD book writing expertise.

From Ellie:

Thanks to Athena, Mairade and Gus for giving me the chance to continue my flowery adventure in the big smoke and for being oh-so-very patient with me. Thank you to my dad, Jamie Jauncey, for all of the advice and support he has given us and reading, re-reading and reading all over again. To my Granny Liz, I hope she can see what we've created. To my mum, Carrie Ede, for making me realise that I love working with flowers and teaching me all she knows. Olly Davy, for keeping us so deliciously fed on those endless nights spent writing, your love and support and for your great attention to detail in the written word. Sarah, Nicky, Sophie, Anna and Jake for their constant encouragement and always being interested in The Flower Appreciation Society.

NOTES

NOTES

WEBSITE:

www.theflowerappreciationsociety.co.uk

TWITTER AND INSTAGRAM:

@flowersociety
#flowerappreciation

FACEBOOK:

www.facebook.com/flowersociety